Mastering Primary Design and Technology

Mastering Primary Teaching series

Edited by Judith Roden and James Archer

The *Mastering Primary Teaching* series provides an insight into the core principles underpinning each of the subjects of the Primary National Curriculum, thereby helping student teachers to 'master' the subjects. This in turn will enable new teachers to share this mastery in their teaching. Each book follows the same sequence of chapters, which has been specifically designed to assist trainee teachers to capitalize on opportunities to develop pedagogical excellence. These comprehensive guides introduce the subject and help trainees know how to plan and teach effective and inspiring lessons that make learning irresistible. Examples of children's work and case studies are included to help exemplify what is considered to be best and most innovative practice in primary education. The series is written by leading professionals, who draw on their years of experience to provide authoritative guides to the primary curriculum subject areas.

Also available in the series

Mastering Primary English, Wendy Jolliffe and David Waugh

Mastering Primary Languages, Paula Ambrossi and Darnelle Constant-Shepherd

Mastering Primary Music, Ruth Atkinson

Mastering Primary Physical Education, Kristy Howells with Alison Carney, Neil Castle and Rich Little

Mastering Primary Science, Amanda McCrory and Kenna Worthington

Forthcoming in the series

Mastering Primary Art and Design, Peter Gregory, Claire March and Suzy Tutchell

Mastering Primary Computing, Graham Parton and Christine Kemp-Hall

Mastering Primary Geography, Anthony Barlow and Sarah Whitehouse

Mastering Primary History, Karin Doull, Christopher Russell and Alison Hales

Mastering Primary Mathematics, Andrew Lamb, Rebecca Heaton and Helen Taylor

Mastering Primary Religious Education, Maria James and Julian Stern

Also available from Bloomsbury

Developing Teacher Expertise, edited by Margaret Sangster

Readings for Reflective Teaching in Schools, edited by Andrew Pollard

Reflective Teaching in Schools, Andrew Pollard

Mastering Primary Design and Technology

Gill Hope

BLOOMSBURY ACADEMIC
LONDON • NEW YORK • OXFORD • NEW DELHI • SYDNEY

BLOOMSBURY ACADEMIC
Bloomsbury Publishing Plc
50 Bedford Square, London, WC1B 3DP, UK
29 Earlsfort Terrace, Dublin 2, Ireland

BLOOMSBURY, BLOOMSBURY ACADEMIC and the Diana logo are trademarks of
Bloomsbury Publishing Plc

First published in Great Britain 2018
Reprinted 2019, 2020 (twice)

© Gill Hope, 2018

Gill Hope has asserted her right under the Copyright, Designs and
Patents Act, 1988, to be identified as Author of this work.

For legal purposes the Acknowledgements on p. xvi constitute an extension
of this copyright page.

Cover design by Anna Berzovan
Cover image © iStock (miakievy / molotovcoketail)

All rights reserved. No part of this publication may be reproduced or transmitted
in any form or by any means, electronic or mechanical, including photocopying,
recording, or any information storage or retrieval system, without prior
permission in writing from the publishers.

Bloomsbury Publishing Plc does not have any control over, or responsibility for,
any third-party websites referred to or in this book. All internet addresses given in
this book were correct at the time of going to press. The author and publisher
regret any inconvenience caused if addresses have changed or sites have ceased
to exist, but can accept no responsibility for any such changes.

A catalogue record for this book is available from the British Library.
A catalog record for this book is available from the Library of Congress.

ISBN: HB: 978-1-4742-9536-9
PB: 978-1-4742-9537-6
ePDF: 978-1-4742-9538-3
ePub: 978-1-4742-9539-0

Series: Mastering Primary Teaching

Typeset by Deanta Global Publishing Services, Chennai, India
Printed and bound in Great Britain

To find out more about our authors and books visit www.bloomsbury.com
and sign up for our newsletters.

To my grandchildren:

Our Canterbury girls

Frankie, aged 4 and three-quarters, who uses technology to solve everyday problems and has such wonderful ideas about everything.

Ella, who was born in October 2016, at the beginning of the writing of this book, and who makes herself busy exploring the potential of the technology in every cupboard she can get into.

Our Shetland family

Jack, just 2, whose safe arrival and the health of his Mummy was only possible through the advances of modern medical technology.

Lily, who arrived the week before the first draft of this book was completed in May 2017.

Contents

List of Figures	viii
List of Tables	x
Series Editors' Foreword	xi
How to Use This Book	xiv
Acknowledgements	xvi
Introduction	**1**
Glossary	**5**
1 **An Introduction to Primary Design and Technology**	7
2 **Current Developments in Design and Technology**	21
3 **Design and Technology as an Irresistible Activity**	45
4 **Design and Technology as a Practical Activity**	67
5 **Skills to Develop in Design and Technology**	93
6 **Children's Ideas – Promoting Curiosity**	113
7 **Assessing Children in Design and Technology**	133
8 **Practical Issues**	149
Bibliography	165
Index	168

List of Figures

1.1	Tool use by another primate	12
1.2	Defining design and technology	13
1.3	The Design and Technology Association's 'Star diagram'	15
2.1	How technology has transformed landscape on Tyneside	36
2.2	Neolithic technology in Orkney	37
2.3	Canals	38
3.1	Middleton's model of seeking a design solution	49
3.2	Kimbell's model of designing	51
3.3	Interaction between mind and hand	51
3.4	The dimensions of design capability	52
3.5	Rogers and Clare's design spiral	52
3.6	Frosty's problem and Icy's solution as worked out by Jason	54
3.7	Why not Boots rather than Slippers?	58
3.8	Planticrubs	60
3.9	Greenhouse made from recycled plastic bottles	61
4.1	A large toy challenging scale using a construction kit	70
4.2	Viking boat: Looks nice but *not* design and technology	73
4.3	Stable frame structures	75
4.4	Shell structures: Vehicles made from recycled packaging	75
4.5	Coil pots: Correct and incorrect joining	76
4.6	A very simple mechanism suitable for Key Stage 1	77
4.7	Hinge mechanisms for use in a greetings card	78
4.8	This mechanism enables reverse motion	78
4.9	A linear to rotary converter	79
4.10	Puppets/toys employing levers: Arms moving	79
4.11	Puppets/toys employing levers: Arms and legs moving	80
4.12	Two examples of wheel attachments	80
4.13	Cam mechanism made by Year 6 boy and Year 4–5 group	81

List of Figures ix

4.14	Model of carousel ride using gears	82
4.15	Pneumatics used to create a moving picture	82
4.16	A toy involving hydraulics part-way through construction	83
4.17	Batik method for children	86
4.18	Two examples of textile products by Year 5 pupils	87
4.19	Finger knitting a belt	88
4.20	Modelling ideas in one medium that will be made in another	89
4.21	Key Stage 2 children can use construction kits to design vehicles with moving parts	90
5.1	Toddlers Jack (a) and Frankie (b) explore fitting small objects inside larger ones	102
5.2	A bit of hasty mending and the toy will sit in his car without it toppling over	104
5.3	Using recycled and/or reclaimed resources	107
5.4	Concept map for reflective activity	108
5.5	Two examples of student responses to the task of expanding Figure 5.4	109
6.1	From unawareness to active investigation in less than five months	114
6.2	Ella's pull-along toy	124
6.3	A pull-along toy that bounces as it moves along	125
6.4	A view across a bridge and the entrance to The Lowry, both at Salford, Greater Manchester	127
7.1	Planning and assessment cycle	134
7.2	Instructions for flow diagram to enable pupils to track their progress through a project	145
8.1	The Design and Technology Association Expert Subject Advisory Group's 'jigsaw diagram'	150

List of Tables

1.1	Reflection on personal experiences of designing and making	8
1.2	The knowledge, skills and dispositions of design and technology capability	19
2.1	Key Stage 1 Science	33
2.2	Lower Key Stage 2 Science	33
2.3	Upper Key Stage 2 Science	34
2.4	A planning grid for cross-curricular work	40
3.1	What I don't like about teaching design and technology	62
4.1	Three design briefs: how well do they score on the 'star diagram'?	71
7.1	Where Grainger et al. (2004) found that creative teaching is likely to flourish	137
7.2	John's scale for assessing the development of independent working in design and technology	139
7.3	Excerpt from the design and technology Progression Framework	143
7.4	Suggested format for recording linking skills across subjects	146

Series Editors' Foreword

A long and varied experience of working with beginner and experienced teachers in primary schools has informed this series since its conception. Over the last thirty years there have been many changes in practice in terms of teaching and learning in primary and early years education. Significantly, since the implementation of the first National Curriculum in 1989 the aim has been to bring best practice in primary education to all state schools in England and Wales. As time has passed, numerous policy decisions have altered the detail and emphasis of the delivery of the primary curriculum. However, there has been little change in the belief that pupils in the primary and early years phases of education should receive a broad, balanced curriculum based on traditional subjects.

Recent OFSTED subject reports and notably the Cambridge Primary Review indicate that, rather than the ideal being attained, in many schools the emphasis on English and mathematics has not only depressed the other subjects of the primary curriculum, but also narrowed the range of strategies used for the delivery of the curriculum. The amount of time allocated to subject sessions in Initial Teacher Education (ITE) courses has dramatically reduced which may also account for this narrow diet in pedagogy.

The vision for this series of books arose out of our many years of experience with student teachers. As a result, we believe that the series is well designed to equip trainee and beginner teachers to master the art of teaching in the primary phase. This series of books aims to introduce current and contemporary practices associated with the whole range of subjects within the Primary National Curriculum and religious education. It also goes beyond this by providing beginner teachers with the knowledge and understanding required to achieve mastery of each subject. In doing so, each book in the series highlights contemporary issues such as assessment and inclusion which are the key areas that even the most seasoned practitioner is still grappling with in light of the introduction of the new primary curriculum.

Readers will find great support within each one of these books. Each book in the series will inform and provide the opportunity for basic mastery of each of the subjects, namely English, mathematics, science, physical education, music, history, geography, design and technology, computing, art and design, languages and religious education. They will discover the essence of each subject in terms of its philosophy, knowledge and skills. Readers will also be inspired by the enthusiasm for each subject revealed by the subject authors who are experts in their field. They will discover many and varied strategies for making each subject 'come alive' for their pupils and they should become more confident about teaching across the whole range of subjects represented in the primary and early years curriculum.

Primary teaching in the state sector is characterized by a long history of pupils being taught the whole range of the primary curriculum by one teacher. Although some schools may employ specialists to deliver some subjects of the curriculum, notably physical education, music or science, for example, it is more usual for the whole curriculum to be delivered to a class by their class teacher. This places a potentially enormous burden on beginner teachers no matter which route they have taken to enter teaching. The burden is especially high on those entering through employment-based routes and for those who aim to become inspiring primary teachers. There is much to learn!

The term 'mastery' relates to knowledge and understanding of a subject which incorporates the 'how' of teaching as well as the 'what'. Although most entrants to primary teaching will have some experience of the primary curriculum as a pupil, very few will have experienced the breadth of the curriculum or may have any understanding of the curriculum which reflects recent trends in teaching and learning within the subject. The primary curriculum encompasses a very broad range of subjects each of which has its own knowledge base, skills and ways of working. Unsurprisingly, very few new entrants into the teaching profession hold mastery of all the interrelated subjects. Indeed for the beginner teacher it may well be many years before full mastery of all aspects of the primary curriculum is achieved. The content of the primary curriculum has changed significantly, notably in some foundation subjects, such as history and music. So although beginner teachers might hold fond memories of these subjects from their own experience of primary education, the content of these subjects may well have changed significantly over time and may incorporate different emphases.

This series, Mastering Primary Teaching, aims to meet the needs of those who, reflecting the desire for mastery over each subject, want to know more. This is a tall order. Nevertheless, we believe that the pursuit of development should always be rewarded, which is why we are delighted to have so many experts sharing their well-developed knowledge and passion for the subjects featured in each book. The vision for this series is to provide support for those who are beginning their teaching career, who may not feel fully secure in their subject knowledge, understanding or skill. In addition, the series also aims to provide a reference point for beginner teachers to consult repeatedly over time to support them in the important art of teaching.

Intending primary teachers, in our experience, have a thirst for knowledge about the subject that they will be teaching. They want to 'master' new material and ideas in a range of subjects. Teaching the primary curriculum can be one of the most rewarding experiences. We believe that this series will help beginner teachers to unlock the primary curriculum in a way that ensures they establish themselves as confident primary practitioners.

Judith Roden
James Archer
June 2017

How to Use This Book

This book is one of twelve books that together help form a truly innovative series that is aimed to support your development. Each book follows the same format and chapter sequence. There is an emphasis throughout the book on providing information about the teaching and learning of design and technology. You will find a wealth of information within each chapter that will help you to understand the issues, problems and opportunities that teaching the subject can provide you as a developing practitioner in the subject. Crucially, each chapter provides opportunities for you to reflect upon important points linked to your development in order that you may master the teaching of design and technology. As a result it helps you to develop your confidence in the teaching of primary design and technology. There really is something for everyone within each chapter.

Each chapter has been carefully designed to help you to develop your knowledge of the subject systematically and as a result contains key features. Chapter objectives clearly signpost the content of each chapter and these will help you to familiarize yourself with important aspects of the subject and will orientate you in preparation for reading the chapter. The regular 'pause for thought' points offer questions and activities for you to reflect on important aspects of the subject. Each 'pause for thought' provides you with an opportunity to enhance your learning beyond merely reading the chapter. These will sometimes ask you to consider your own experience and what you already know about the teaching of the subject. Others will require you to critique aspects of good practice presented as case studies or research. To benefit fully from reading this text, you need to be an active participant. Sometimes you are asked to make notes on your response to questions and ideas and then to revisit these later on in your reading. While it would be possible for you to skip through the opportunities for reflection or to give only cursory attention to the questions and activities which aim to facilitate deeper reflection than might otherwise be the case we strongly urge you to engage with the 'pause for thought' activities. It is our belief that it is through these moments that most of your transformational learning will occur, as a result of engaging in this book. At the end of each chapter, you will find a summary of main points from the chapter along with suggestions for further reading.

We passionately believe that learners of all ages learn best when they work with others, so we would encourage you, if possible to work with another person, sharing your ideas and perspectives. The book also would be ideal for group study within a university or school setting.

This book has been authored by Gill Hope who is an experienced and highly regarded professional in her subject area. She is a strong voice within the primary design and technology community. By reading this book you will be able to benefit from her rich knowledge, understanding and experience. When using this, ensure that you are ready to learn from one of the greats in primary design and technology.

Acknowledgements

Thank you to:

Eric Parkinson, retired principal lecturer at Canterbury Christ Church University for the use of his '5 Ms' in Chapter 3;

Willy Adams, Educational Resources, Design and Technology Association, for permission to quote work published by the Design and Technology Association;

John Rapley, Design and Technology teacher at The Meadows School, Southborough, Kent, for his help and permission to use his materials in Chapter 7;

Gerry Wetheral, retired head-teacher at Halfway Houses Primary School who gave consent for me to use data, scans of children's drawings and photographs of their work for purposes of research and writing;

Students on Initial Education Courses at Canterbury Christ Church University who gave permission to use photographs of their investigations into design and technology for teaching and writing purposes;

My son and daughter-in-law, Ralph and Sabina Hope, and my daughter and son-in-law, Rachel and Richard Shucksmith, for permission to include references to and photographs of my grandchildren.

All photographs are copyright of Dr. Gill Hope, except where stated.

Introduction

Welcome to this book about design and technology in the primary school!

Recently, I was showing some old family photographs to my four-year-old granddaughter, Frankie. 'This is my Grandma's mother,' I said, showing her a photo of 'Old Gran' in her long skirt and pudding basin hat, the fashion of the 1920s, standing in a cottage garden. The house had no electricity; it was lit by gas lamps and heated by coal fires, had a copper for boiling clothes and a mangle for getting out the excess water; there was a meat safe outside the backdoor to keep it fresh overnight, and an outside privy (on the back of the house, an improvement on the house she lived in when she was first married which had it at the bottom of the garden). I know all this because my great-aunt lived in the same house with the same amenities when I was a child in the 1950s. My grandma had no lighting at all in the upstairs in her house. She took a candle to bed and left an oil lamp burning on the stairs. My great-aunt and grandma were the only two of eight children to survive beyond age five.

The technological advances that have been made in the past 100 years have vastly improved our lives in the Westernized world. In the next 100 years, another (probably more) technological revolution(s) will have taken place. We are still only at the beginning of the digital revolution. Medical research has made more discoveries that can be fully implemented at present. Ways to cut our dependence on oil and other fossil fuels through green energy are beginning to become viable. Reducing and recycling our wastage and carbon emissions need addressing urgently or we might make our planet uninhabitable before we can apply the technology to fix it. The benefits of advanced technology need to spread to all people across the planet, without ruining their environments or their social and cultural heritages.

This is why I believe it to be essential for all children to learn about technology and how to design technological solutions to the needs of all peoples, understanding our dependence on the health of the planet and our interrelatedness with all life that shares Earth with us. It is a Big Ask. Teachers, your contribution counts!

I hope that by reading this book you will gain some of my passion and enthusiasm for the subject. Teaching design and technology is so much fun – where else can you go to work and play with paper, card, wood, textiles or food alongside a bunch of little people as committed to making learning fun as you are? Design and technology provides a real-life context for English, mathematics and science, and links are easily made with history and geography. However – it must be real design and technology, not just 'craft' or 'making things' and it must *not* get confused with art (even though both subjects have the word 'design' attached to them). This book will discuss the intellectual and practical challenges and opportunities that design and technology offers to primary school pupils.

NOTE 1: Throughout this book, you will find that the subject is always called 'design and technology', never abbreviated to 'd&t' or 'dt'. The danger of using such abbreviations is in forgetting what they stand for. In a book whose intention is to improve classroom practitioners' understanding of subject and improve their teaching, it is imperative that this does not happen.

NOTE 2: All names of children, students, teachers and teaching assistants have been changed throughout the book, except for John Rapley and The Meadows School, Southborough, Kent.

Chapter synopses

Chapter 1 will introduce you to the area of learning that we call 'design and technology' and present you with a definition of the subject. This will lead into a consideration of why it should be taught and its importance to children's learning and development.

Chapter 2 discusses current developments in teaching design and technology, focusing on the National Curriculum for England (2014). Chapter 3 describes the current developments in design and technology and the new National Curriculum for England (2014). The focus is on England because that is where this series of books is being published. However, the principles of design and technology, the knowledge and skills children acquire remain true wherever the subject is taught. This is illustrated by a brief discussion of other countries' curricula for design and technology. Readers from other countries are advised to refer to their own regional, state or national curricula but may find it helpful, in order to follow the arguments in this chapter and the rest of the book, to also download this English curriculum document.

I am often asked 'Why do you teach design and technology?' and my immediate response is 'Because it's so much fun!' Chapter 3 not only asserts that children enjoy the subject but that they deserve to enjoy high-quality design and technology. To that end, the basic foundational thinking that underpins the subject is explained. If pupils are not enjoying the subject, maybe what they are experiencing is not the real thing?

Chapter 4 focuses on the activity that most characterizes design and technology: making things. The range of areas into which this making activity can be divided are discussed in detail. Examples are given and pictures provided to enable the reader to see what kind of things can be made by primary-aged pupils. The capability that they develop with tools and equipment with a range of materials, components and ingredients are discussed as the chapter progresses.

This depth of discussion of the practical aspects of design and technology means that Chapter 5, which is dedicated to discussing skills, can focus on those that underlie the making. Parkinson's '5 Ms' (making, modelling, mending, manipulating and modifying) are used as the basis for this discussion.

Chapter 6 tackles the balance between imagination and realism – the conflict that must always exist in the mind of a creative designer. The product must function well for its intended user but the designer needs to be able to apply imagination and flair to the design of it. Young children specialize in fantasy, they can think of a multitude of ideas and possibilities and imagine all the parts that cannot be made from the materials at hand. Older ones may even demand of themselves and their work a realism that is often beyond their capability to create.

The assessment of pupils' capability is the subject of Chapter 7. The basis for this chapter is taken as assessment for learning: formative assessment that will enable pupils and teacher to know where their next step should take them.

Finally, Chapter 8 discusses practical issues that occur, often at a whole-school level: minimum requirements for teaching the subject adequately, health and safety, inclusion and diversity, ending with the proposition of how to respond if asked to lead the subject within the school and the support that is available for the reader to be able to do so successfully.

Along the way, you will:

- Learn how design and technology contributes to children's learning;
- Consider what technology has done for us – its importance throughout history and across the globe;
- Understand how learning to design technological products can develop children's learning and development.
- Begin to appreciate the importance of teaching the subject well and make a commitment to do so.

Each chapter has several 'Pause for thought' activities. You should do just that: think about the questions and, if possible, write down your responses and/or discuss these with colleagues. These may be based on a case study, an online resource or an example of children's work.

At the end of each chapter is a list of Recommended Readings for your understanding of a specific point within the chapter and has been chosen to develop your thinking. Each of these readings is available online at the time of publication and the web address has been provided. The bibliography includes full references to all texts referred to throughout the book.

What about the Early Years?

Although I worked for many years in a First School which catered to pupils aged 4–9 years, and I was Year 1 leader for the last seven years of working there, I have not included the Early Years Foundation Stage (EYFS), that is, children younger than 5 years, in this book. The reason is simply that 'design and technology' as a subject does not occur in the EYFS curriculum and in many countries children do not start formal education until age 6 or even 7. Technology comes under Understanding of the World in the EYFS and although young pupils in nurseries, preschools, kindergartens and reception classes worldwide use design skills while making products, there is much more emphasis on imagining possibilities and much less emphasis on purpose, function and authenticity than in the curricula for the primary school age range. This is not to denigrate the contribution that children's imagination makes to later development but rather a recognition of the more holistic nature of early learning and experience.

Resources to support designing in the Early Years can be purchased from the Design and Technology Association through https://www.data.org.uk/resource-shop/early-years-foundation-stage/

Glossary

To make sure you will be able to follow the arguments throughout the book, here is a brief glossary of how I use key words:

Artefact A product that can be used by someone (e.g. table, cup, bag). Artefacts can include tools (a hammer is both an artefact and a tool) or components such as nails, but we do not usually describe food as an artefact, so your dinner is not an artefact, even if it includes your best hand-made pierogi with vanilla-flavoured curd cheese and cherries.

Design (verb) To imagine and create ideas for something to be made.

Design (noun) An idea for something that might be made that has been worked out in some detail perhaps by drawing, making a model or using a computer.

Design brief The design problem or opportunity that is presented to the designer (e.g. asking pupils to design suitable packaging for an Easter Egg that will appeal to a child). The design brief must include a specific user and purpose for the product that is to be made.

Design criteria The potential and limitations of the design solution, that is, what it must/could/should do or not do (in designing packaging for an Easter Egg, the egg must fit inside securely and the packaging must be springtime-themed).

Iteration/iterative A cyclical process. In design and technology this means that designing and evaluating continue throughout the whole process of planning and making a product.

Model (noun) Anything made in one medium that represents something that exists or will exist in another. For instance, a model of a boat made from a plastic bottle. A design drawing is also a model because it exists as lines on paper which represent something that will be made of real materials; so is a computer simulation (hence 'computer model').

Model (verb) To develop ideas for a design solution. Modelling can include working things out in your head as well as on paper, on-screen or with materials such as paper, card, wood or fabric. The result is more likely to be a prototype than the finished product.

Product The final outcome of designing a functional technological solution that satisfies the design brief and its criteria, made using authentic materials.

Prototype The first attempt at creating a working solution to a design problem. It might be in different (perhaps cheaper) materials than the final product or lack the finish or even be just part of the final design solution.

System A unified, interacting collection of artefacts or mechanisms. A pair of jeans is a system as it includes a zipper and button as well as the fabric pieces. A hydraulic system is made of chambers, a piston and connecting piping and may be just one of the systems in a product such as a car.

Technology Anything and everything designed and made by humans to solve or enhance human life, that is, the whole of the humanly made world from buildings to clothes to cookery to vehicles to computers. Note: the word is commonly used just for hi-tech products but this is misleading.

Tool A product that can be used to make other products (e.g. hammer, spoon, computer).

Note on age ranges in English primary schools for readers from other countries: *Although frequently attending nursery or reception classes on-site, formal schooling officially starts at age 5. Pupils aged 5–7 years are in Key Stage 1 and pupils aged 7–11 years are in Key Stage 2 (sub-divided into 'lower' and 'upper'), after which they transfer to secondary school. These three age divisions are used throughout the book. Readers from beyond the UK may be surprised to learn that these do not apply to Scotland or Northern Ireland.*

Chapter 1
An Introduction to Primary Design and Technology

Chapter objectives

- To consider the central role of technology in human development and society;
- To celebrate the curiosity and creativity that underpins solving design problems;
- To outline the contribution of design and technology to children's learning and development;
- To persuade readers of the importance of high-quality teaching of design and technology.

Introduction

This chapter begins (by way of priority) by defining 'design and technology' as a curriculum subject and clarifying its distinction from both art and science. The subject must not be reduced to simply 'making things' or 'craft by another name'. Designing technology is purposeful; its essential goal is to satisfy a human need or want (sometimes even creating a want!) through creating objects that people can use. These can range from the very tiny (e.g. a microchip) to the huge (a whole landscape of paddy fields). Wherever you are on Planet Earth, you are surrounded by things or systems or environments that have been made or affected by the making of objects by and for humans.

Making things seems to be at the very heart of what it is to be human, part of our basic make-up as a curious and creative species, which means that the opportunity to develop these skills in a practical context should form a rich part of every child's education – and part of their educational entitlement is to be taught design and technology by knowledgeable, enthusiastic and committed teachers.

This chapter ends with a brief overview of the structure of the book, explaining the contribution of each chapter to providing a framework for developing expertise and confidence in teaching design and technology.

> **Pause for thought**
>
> Already? Well, yes, because it's too easy to just skip over the first few pages of an introduction.
> Think about, discuss and write down your ideas in answer to these questions:
>
> - What does design and technology mean to you?
> - How does it relate to science?
> - How does it relate to the 'craft' side of art?
> - How does 'design and technology' relate to the world of hi-tech computerization?
> - What have you seen of design and technology in school?
> - What are your memories of learning design and technology when you were in school?

Case Study 1.1 records a conversation between Alek and Maria, two students on a part-time undergraduate Initial Teacher Education course. Their tutor had asked the group to look back on their own experiences of design and technology. You might like to spend a few moments reflecting on your own experiences of designing and making things, both at school and in your own time.

Draw and complete a table like the one shown as Table 1.1, reflecting on your own experiences of designing and making:

Table 1.1 Reflection on personal experiences of designing and making

Things I can remember making in school:	Things I can remember making at home / at a club:	Things I have seen children making:	Things I enjoy making as an adult:

If possible, share your memories with a friend or a small group. How do your lists compare? What bigger issues have come out of your discussion? Which of these would be part of design and technology? Use the 'unique characteristics' list in this chapter to help you decide.

All activities that create a product that has both a practical function and a purpose are likely to be the ones that qualify as design and technology. Products that are

An Introduction to Primary Design and Technology

decorative or express ideas and/or emotions but lack a practical function probably fall into the remit of art and design. Activities that explore the way the world works but do not create a product that someone can use, come under science.

However, these boundaries can be blurred, as illustrated by Case Study 1.1 which reports on Maria and Alek's discussion.

CASE STUDY 1.1 Reflecting on your own experience

Maria's list:

Things I can remember making in school:	Things I can remember making at home / at a club:	Things I have seen children making:	Things I enjoy making as an adult:
Slippers in Year 6 Electric circuits	Puppets	Pots for Mother's Day Models of Tudor houses	Paper flowers

At this point she is stumped and looks over to see why her friend Alek is still writing. Is it a boy thing? Do boys just do more of this stuff when they are little, she wonders. Alek stops and looks at her list. He's clearly not impressed.

Alek: You haven't listed any foodstuffs or anything made with construction kits.
Maria: Mm. I couldn't really think of much. You put those?
Alek: Yes. I used to play with Lego all the time, so I put that under the 'home' list.
Maria: What do you think about the pots for Mother's Day? I'm not sure if it was in an art lesson or design and technology.
Alek: Don't know. Could be either, I guess. But I'm really not sure about your paper flowers. Do they have a practical purpose or are they just pretty? Also, I've seen children making puppets in art.
Maria: Puppets have a real purpose as props for a play, don't they? But I guess I agree about the flowers. I don't really do anything else like making stuff.
Alek: You cook! Your pasta sauces are amazing!
Maria: That's because my gran's Italian and she used to look after me a lot when I was little.
Alek: And you make cards. The one you made for Sam's birthday was amazing.
Maria: Oh yes, I should have put that on my list. Children make cards too, don't they? Christmas cards.
Alek: And you knitted your sister a little hat for her baby.
Maria: Can you teach children to knit? They do sewing don't they? Is that d&t too? I made a pinny at school, then we had to wear them for Home Ec. the next term.

Both Maria and Alek had memories of making things at school but were uncertain whether these things were really design and technology or something else. They were especially confused between design and technology and art and design. Maria had also listed 'electric circuits' but had not considered what these might be used for; one important aspect of design and technology is its practical purpose.

Alek and Maria had just started to identify other creative things that Maria did. Although Alek was sure that something that is simply decorative (Maria's paper flowers) should be considered as art rather than design and technology, they were confused about the pots and the puppets. Their tutor then joined the discussion and looked at Maria's list. She classed the electric circuits as a scientific investigation to provide pupils with essential knowledge that they could incorporate into their products (a 'Focused Practical Task').

She explained that making models of Tudor houses might class as a practical activity in a history lesson (although a colleague who taught history had said he would class it as poor teaching in his subject too) but there was no real designing happening. Maria asked the tutor if it could be improved since it seemed like a good cross-curricular project. The tutor smiled and said 'Think about it!' as she headed off to look at another pair's list.

We will come back to that challenge at the end of this chapter.

What is design and technology?

There have been many attempts at defining 'design and technology', but I find it helpful to think of its subject matter as 'designing technology': devising and creating something practical to satisfy a human need or want. Designing technology always has purpose. It has produced all of the objects surrounding you: in the room in which you are now sitting, what you are wearing, how you will get home or to work, what you will eat later today (and how it was sourced, prepared and sold) or it may be designing a tool to enable someone to create all of these things. Technological production always has by-products. Children nowadays are aware of its effects on the environment and that we should reuse or recycle things we no longer want or need.

In everyday life, the word 'technology' is frequently used as shorthand for 'digital technology' or 'computer technology' and often when people ask me what I do, their immediate response to the word 'technology' is to express their opinion on or capability with computers. I think this is partly because the development of technology has always been about inventing something new. Today it is in the world of electronics, a hundred years ago it would have been seeing the first car driving through your village (one of my father's childhood memories), nearly two centuries ago it would have been the building of the first railways, and so on back through time. The 'new-fangled' can be exciting, opening up possibilities, or threatening the known, secure and comfortable, depending on your point of view.

Basically, technology is everything designed and made by humans

It includes:

- *Feeding ourselves:* spears, bows and arrows, guns for hunting; ploughs, harnesses, sickles, balers, combine harvesters; pestles, querns, mills, baskets and pots for baking, brewing, stewing; preserving through drying, salting, boiling with sugar, chilling, freezing; serving in bowls, plates, cups; eating with spoons, forks, chop sticks; washing up, composting or disposing of leftovers.
- *Keeping warm:* fire-making: campfires, braziers, chimneys, oil lamps, gas fires, electric heaters, central heating; clothes: furs and leather, textiles (felted, woven and knitted), fibres from plants, animals and petrochemicals, spinning wheels, spinning jennies, hand looms, steam-powered weaving sheds; needles and pins for sewing, knitting, crochet plus scissors to cut the yarn and the cloth; shelters and houses made from grass, leather, felt, wood, stone, bricks, concrete, organized into villages, towns, cities with infrastructure such as water, power and transport.
- *Moving about:* sleds, skates, skis, snowboards; harnesses, saddles, stirrups, saddlebags; wheels: carts, chariots, carriages, trains, bicycles, cars, lorries; boats: rafts, canoes, paddles, dug-outs, coracles, fishing boats, yachts, tall ships, liners, cruisers, aircraft carriers, tankers.
- *Defending ourselves:* from predators and each other (oh, dear!), which has led to the development of the parts of the technological spectrum we would rather forget about: sticks, stones, bows and arrows, catapults, guns, cannons, bombs, WMDs, H bombs; shields, gas masks, air-raid shelters, nuclear basements; the whole sad litany of the arms race with its dehumanizing of the enemy to rationalize our response rate.

The more you think, the longer becomes the list – and even the categories of lists.

> **Pause for thought**
>
> Let's turn to a happier topic: relaxation! Write as full a list as you can of all the technology involved in sitting, sleeping, home and mobile entertainment and in your favourite leisure activities.

In fact, practically every object that humans use nowadays has been processed or manufactured in some way, using tools or machines. One of the unique and radical things that humans do is to make tools to make tools.

Chimpanzees are famed tool-users and have been observed adapting to and improving on intentionally collected or reserved objects, but no other species besides hominids have been observed making a tool that can be used to make another tool.

Figure 1.1 Tool use by another primate

This ability to take one conceptual step back, as it were, is unique to our species. It seems to be a step too far for any creature with a brain much smaller or less complex than that of the *hominid* group. Many monkeys and some birds will find and use sticks to reach things. Figure 1.1 shows a gibbon at Wingham Wildlife Park, Kent, choosing and using a stick to reach nuts that had landed outside his enclosure. He could see the potential of an already existing object but could not have designed and made something more effective, something even as simple as a stick with a hook at the end. However, some crows have been observed bending sticks to get food from bird-feeders.

Once *Homo habilis* was making fire, cooking food and discovering that flint could be worked much more easily if first heated, our distant ancestors were off on the long path of technological experimentation, discovery and invention that led to that long string of physical, cognitive, linguistic and social changes that brought us to where we are now and which has enabled us to create the complex world in which we live, to reflect on our achievements and to seek to create improvements.

Yet we are increasingly aware of what a mess we have made of the planet through our technology. Human technological activity is believed to be responsible for climate change, pollution, mismanagement of resources and more. If there is any way we can get ourselves back out of this mess, it has to be through technological change on a global scale. Our pupils are very aware of these issues; they know about climate change and worry about it too – what kind of world are they inheriting from us? If they have children, what are their chances? These big issues will not go away. We cannot pretend that humans have not made huge mistakes and continue to do so. The problem is that we rarely realize it until afterwards; hindsight is a wonderful thing, as they say. As teachers, we have the potential to help create a generation of problem-solvers; those who will look for and encourage innovative ways to solve the challenges and demands of their future. These problems will be practical as well as intellectual. Design and technology education is well placed to make a major contribution to this need.

The essence of design and technology

All technology is purposefully designed. Even those things that came about completely by accident (and there are not actually very many of these) had to be adapted or improved to make them properly fit for some purpose by their users. Figure 1.2 shows the Design and Technology Association's Memorable Definition for Design and Technology, which helps to differentiate an activity as being design and technology and not art or science (this can be viewed on a product description page at https://www.data.org.uk/shopproducts/are-you-really-teaching-dt-and-dt-principles-guidance/).

The key word is *purpose*. Art is about expressing ideas, observations and emotional response (including the feel-good factor of a pleasing aesthetic). Technology is rather more earthy. We may like our mugs to have a nice shape, colour and decoration but if they do not hold coffee or the handle falls off they are discarded as no longer fit for purpose. Many artists challenge the nature of art by taking technological objects and re-imaging them as art but, in essence, this is no different from painting a still life of fruit, vegetable and meat pie. A cushion cover may be a work of art but we expect the cushion to *function* properly (be comfortable, support our back etc.) and that is an essentially technological characteristic.

An example: I once bought a beautiful, quirky (and expensive) bag from a gallery shop in Lewis, East Sussex. It was urn-shaped and felted from un-dyed fleece but it quickly ended its days being touted around introductory design and technology lectures as an example of an object that was aesthetically pleasing but of no practical use. Basically, it was an art object and not a practical, intended-for-use solution to my

Figure 1.2 Defining design and technology

> Designing and making :
>
> Something for
>
> Somebody for
>
> Some purpose

need for carrying things. It was useless as a bag. It was worse than not waterproof, the felt absorbed water so that even on a damp day all my belongings got soggy. Plus, because of the urn shape, if you put a standard-sized magazine inside it was the devil's own job to get it back out again. My students would be in peals of laughter. How could I have been so stupid to have bought such a ridiculous item? But it looked quirky and different.

> **Pause for thought**
>
> Have you ever bought something that looked good in the shop but failed to meet the need for which you bought it? Have a discussion with friends about this, perhaps over a coffee. You can have a good laugh as well as developing your understanding of the technological need for fitness for purpose that does not apply in the same way to art.

The confusion between art and design and technology is highlighted by students who ask: 'Is clay design and technology or art?' (or a similar question about textiles). The answer is that clay and textiles are *materials* that can be used both in art and in design and technology projects. The difference between design and technology and art is not in what materials are used but in the *purpose of the product*. Design and technology products serve to answer to people's needs and wants in a practical way. Clay can be used to make sculptures (art) as well as crockery (technology); textiles can be used for wall hangings (art) as well as bags, clothes, sails and machine belts (technology). Vases and soft furnishings could be seen as either, depending on your point of view.

One of the differences between designing in art and designing technology is that art allows for a degree of divergence from the brief which cannot be accommodated within technological design – in the end the product must work. Being creative within design and technology is not the same as being divergent and having ideas no one else has thought of. Designing a technological product also requires the rationality of science: when a new technique or a new material is to be tried, the manufacturer wants to know if this is better than what is already in use. For example, just prior to the start of the Industrial Revolution in the Midlands, a group of entrepreneurs and scientists met monthly to discuss their technological problems and the new scientific developments. This group became known as the Lunar Society and included Erasmus Darwin and Josiah Wedgewood (the two grandfathers of Charles Darwin). Wedgewood was not there for the social chit-chat. He was there to glean all he could about the chemistry of glazing, including picking the brains of members of similar groups in Germany with whom the Lunar Society corresponded. It was no use him having wonderful creative ideas for new ceramics if he could not get the glaze to stick to the pot.

Figure 1.3 shows the Design and Technology Association's 'Star diagram' that indicates the six essential aspects of designing and making a product that every

Figure 1.3 The Design and Technology Association's 'Star diagram'. This can be viewed on a product description page at https://www.data.org.uk/shopproducts/are-you-really-teaching-dt-and-dt-principles-guidance/

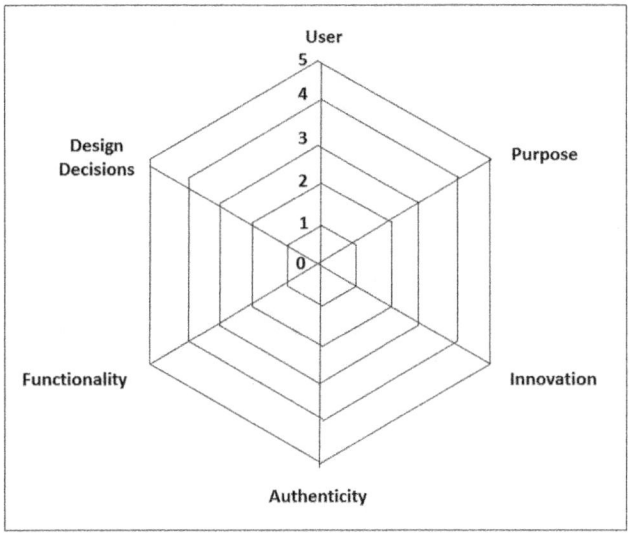

design and technology project should contain. It can be used for planning a project, for assessment of pupil attainment and also to support pupils in self-assessment of the way in which their design ideas are shaping up. Not all projects will provide opportunities for pupils to achieve maximum points on all scales but good long-term planning should ensure that the opportunities are there across the whole year. The way these six principles underpin design and technology are explained in 'Characteristics of a genuine D&T experience within the school curriculum: Principles for guiding and evaluating practice' listed in the Recommended Reading list for this chapter.

> **Pause for thought**
>
> How does this diagram map to the aims and purposes, as well as the details of content, of the curriculum followed in schools in which you will be / are teaching?

Why should design and technology be taught?

Human society and civilization have been built on our invention, adoption and adaptation of technology to improve our lives and make our surroundings more agreeable. Technology is all around us. Every man-made object we see, touch, hear, smell or taste has been designed and made by somebody. Society needs the designers of the future who will be able to create effective solutions to the needs and wants of individuals, groups, nations and the multinational community.

The skills and abilities required to make successful products need to be learnt, practised and developed in a safe environment. This provides an appreciation of how things are made and how long it might take to become really proficient. Designing and making things oneself enhances the ability to appreciate the skills of others, whether these are friends within a peer group or expert craftspeople from a different generation, place or culture.

Creative activity is essential to human well-being because:

- Designing and making something for oneself is deeply satisfying and develops personal self-confidence and well-being.
- Developing one's own ideas and trying them out develops intelligence, creativity, evaluation, perseverance and problem-solving skills.
- Thinking about the needs of others and designing a solution or product enhances empathy for and understanding of other people, especially when their needs and wants may be quite different from that of the designer.

In the recent past, a view of a 'good education' in primary schools emerged that was narrowed down to the 'basics' of literacy, numeracy and ICT, with a smattering of science, history and geography added in, to better equip them for achieving academic success in secondary school and eventual employment. This view seems to imply the de-valuing of primary education itself, relegating it to providing skills for the structured, exam-led courses of the secondary school.

> ### Pause for thought
>
> Consider for a moment those elements of a child's development that this view of education omits:
>
> - Would an education that does not include the learning of any practical skills adequately prepare children for adult life?
> - How would a lack of hands-on experience of the real world affect children's interaction with each other and their environment?
> - If children's education provides few opportunities to make and weigh up the results of personal choices, how does this impact on the development of independence and the taking of responsibility for their own actions?
> - If this emphasis on instruction and the practice of these 'basic' skills require young children to sit still for extended periods, then does this not contribute to the range of health issues associated with a sedentary lifestyle?

These issues raise the bigger issue:

- What is childhood for?

And, hence,

- What is education of children for?

This is not, of course, an either/or issue. Childhood is both a preparation for the future and a precious time of life to be enjoyed and savoured in its own right. Children deserve an educational experience in our primary schools that both prepares them for the future and enriches their lives as presently experienced.

How can design and technology contribute to a child's learning and development?

Designing and making satisfying products adds to children's sense of well-being and agency. When we are in a state of 'flow' as Csikszentmihalyi (1990) called it, we can lose sense of time and become totally absorbed in what we are doing. This is good for our health as the heart-rate slows and endorphins flow through our bodies. Not only does the creative process itself promote a sense of well-being but so does the sheer satisfaction of having solved a problem, come up with a new way of doing something, learnt a new skill or applied an idea from one area of knowledge to another, plus the joy of making something that can be used by ourselves or someone else. All this adds to a sense of 'can do'; a sense of agency and independence, which is so important for growing children who are hardwired to want to learn to do things for themselves.

The unique characteristics of design and technology can be summarized as:

- *A practical form of knowledge.* Through design and technology, children's minds and hands act on the real-world tools, materials and components to develop products of their own design which satisfy a human need or want. Design and technology harnesses children's love of active, hands-on designing and making. It develops practical capability and hand-skills that encourage self-reliance and independence. The ability to make and mend things contributes to economic security and self-fulfilment.
- *A distinct form of designing:* To be successful, products in design and technology have to work and be appropriate for specified users and uses. Children's thinking focuses on the functionality and usefulness of what they are intending to make. Developing such functional products stimulates the development of skills and capabilities that will help generate solutions for meeting human needs in the home, community and wider world, including technological sustainability;
- *Contributes to personal well-being:* Design and technology meets basic human needs to be creative, autonomous and make personal choices. Children enjoy the challenge of complex high-level practical problem-solving

that combines knowledge, skill and creativity through hands-on activities that children find purposeful, authentic and relevant to their own lives. This 'thought and action' process of complex problem-solving is fundamental to cognitive and neurological development. When designing and making products, children embark on a complex process that combines practical and intellectual skills with an understanding of aesthetic, technical, cultural, health, social, emotional, economic, industrial and environmental issues.

- *Evaluation of existing products and of their own work in progress*: In design and technology, children learn about a wide range of products from the past and present, finding out how things work and how they were made. They learn to look at the made world through 'designer's eyes', to appreciate the craftsmanship involved in making a quality product and become informed and discriminating consumers. They explore their feelings about their own and others' products. Their own ideas and work in progress can be objectively evaluated through the continuous, direct feedback of self-assessment, as well as through input from their peers and their teacher. In return, they learn to offer praise and helpful critique to the ideas, efforts and results of the work of others.

- *Unifying children's learning:* Design and technology draws together many apparently disparate aspects of the curriculum into a single, coherent learning experience that provides continuous opportunities for children to apply and combine learning from across the curriculum, especially science, maths, art and ICT. Scientific understanding and experimental methods are needed to enable children to design and make genuinely functional products, while their artistic skills are used to develop the aesthetic appeal of their products. Mathematical concepts and skills are needed to solve problems of size, shape and fit. A range of essential ICT skills are developed, notably computer-aided design and control technology.

- *Preparation for later life:* Design and technology prepares children to act decisively in an unpredictable, increasingly technology-dominated world. It equips them with the entrepreneurial, practical and social skills needed for everyday life and future employment – skills crucial to their family, community and the nation's economic prosperity and well-being.

Table 1.2 indicates the range of the knowledge, skills and dispositions developed as children's design and technology capabilities increase. For the sake of clarity, design capability and technological capability have been separated but there are clear parallels and overlaps.

Designing technology raises ethical and moral issues. We see this in relation to the big issues of climate change, deforestation, over-fishing, pollution and other aspects of environmental degradation. The speed of technological change across the past hundred years is staggering and appears to be accelerating in many areas of knowledge, transforming people's lives, often for the better but sometimes for the worse. However, this applies at the personal level too. Considering the health and

Table 1.2 The knowledge, skills and dispositions of design and technology capability

	Design capability	Technological capability
Knowledge	Application of prior knowledge to a new problem or design opportunity; Recognition of relevance of both prior and newly acquired knowledge to a new design scenario; Knowing where to seek information that would be relevant to solving the design problem.	Knowing how things work; Understanding and applying relevant scientific principles; Understanding the potential and limitations of materials, tools and artefacts.
Skills	Ability to analyse and identify the core of the problem to be solved; Being able to generate suitable solutions and to transfer those ideas into making a successful product; To share ideas with others through talking, drawing, model-making or using digital tools.	Choosing and using appropriate simple tools to cut, fold, shape, form, join, combine and fit together a range of materials, ingredients and components; Developing gross and fine motor skills together with hand–eye coordination to use tools and fit parts together accurately.
Dispositions	Open-mindedness, creativity, willingness to try something new, taking risks within safe limits; Ability to take on the perspectives of another person, whether collaborator or user.	Working safely with due care and attention to one's own actions and their consequences; Negotiation and cooperation when working with or near others; sharing; Diligence and perseverance when things go wrong or need changing.

safety of others while working involves making choices that reflect the right attitude towards other people. Being able to design and make something for someone else includes developing empathy and learning to respect the needs and wishes of those who may have different circumstances, lifestyles or perspectives from one's own.

Howe, Davies and Ritchie (2001) asserted that children's spiritual sensitivity feeds on experiences such as

- the pleasure derived from being praised by teachers and peers (and in turn identifying the excellence of the work of others);
- the joy and pride of being able to take home something that is well-made, required a lot of effort or represents the mastery of a new skill;
- the sense of awe and wonder when faced with high-quality craftsmanship of any sort, whether something tiny like a piece of exquisite jewellery or the soaring architecture of a cathedral.

Summary

This initial chapter has focused on three major areas:

- the pervasiveness of technology in supporting all aspects of human life;
- the uniqueness of the subject of design and technology and its contribution to children's learning, curiosity and creativity;
- the importance of user, purpose and functionality in designing a technological product.

Reflective question: *Look back over the chapter and try to answer Maria's question to her tutor (see Case Study 1.1). Could the 'Tudor houses' be improved on to include each of the aspects of good design and technology shown on the 'star diagram' depicted in this chapter – or is it impossible? What about ... imagining being a member of the first colonists heading off to the Americas and being faced with hot dry summers and cold snowy winters. There are rocks, trees and rushes around where you have landed. What kind of houses might you build? Does this do better? If so, how and why?*

Recommended reading

The statutory curriculum for your country, state or region. For England this can be found at
   https://www.gov.uk/government/uploads/system/uploads/attachment_data/file/239041/PRIMARY_national_curriculum_-_Design_and_technology.pdf

The South Australian Companion Document for Design and Technology, available
   at http://www.sacsa.sa.edu.au/ATT/%7BF51C47E3-B6F3-4765-83C3-0E27FF5DD952%7D/R-10_Design_&_Tech.pdf

'Characteristics of a genuine D&T experience within the school curriculum: Principles for guiding and evaluating practice' available at https://www.data.org.uk/media/1130/school-curriculum-principles-for-dt.pdf

Chapter 2
Current Developments in Design and Technology

Chapter objectives

- To understand the development of design and technology as a subject in England up to 2014;
- To become acquainted with requirements of the National Curriculum for England 2014;
- To consider the position of food technology and the impact of government concerns about the state of young peoples' health;
- To appreciate how other curriculum subjects relate to children's learning in design and technology.

This chapter discusses the National Curriculum for Design and Technology in England (2014). Some areas of the UK have closely followed the English curriculum but others have not. The Scottish school system is different from that in England and teachers who work near the border need to be aware of both systems. The underlying beliefs about the nature of design and technology are, however, shared by researchers and subject leaders across all four nations of the UK.

The National Curriculum for Design and Technology for England 2014 can be downloaded at https://www.gov.uk/government/uploads/system/uploads/attachment_data/file/239041/PRIMARY_national_curriculum_-_Design_and_technology.pdf

The Design and Technology Association and the Expert Subject Advisory Group (ESAG) for design and technology provides:

- annotated advice and explanatory sheet at https://www.data.org.uk/resource-shop/primary/annotated-programme-of-study-key-messages-advice-and-explanatory-notes-for-schools-pdf-copy/
- Information to clear up a number of misconceptions: https://www.data.org.uk/resource-shop/primary-dt-national-curriculum-2014- myths-and-facts/

Curriculum history in brief

As in any other field of public life, to understand current developments in design and technology it is important to understand what lies behind them. This chapter, therefore, will begin with some history to aid your understanding of the core beliefs about the nature of design and technology held by the community of practice who have been instrumental in developing the subject and whose research and professional knowledge has shaped the National Curriculum for England 2014. Developments in England have influenced the development of design and technology in Canada, Australia, South Africa and many other parts of the world. Through international conferences, researchers, academics and policymakers met, exchanged ideas and created a shared understanding of what constitutes the subject.

The best source of information about the evolution of the design and technology curriculum in England in the period 1988–2014 is in the STEM e-library. This can be found at https://www.stem.org.uk/elibrary/collection/3200

The principles underlying good design and technology pedagogy were established in the 1980s through research in secondary schools. The Assessment and Performance Unit commissioned a team at Goldsmiths College, London University led by Richard Kimbell, who already had a track record in technological design research and publication. Kimbell and his team assessed the design capability of 15,000 15-year-olds across England and this came to be regarded as a seminal, foundational piece of research (Kimbell et.al. 1991, p. 20).

Before the introduction of design and technology, primary schools taught 'craft', which might include anything from embroidered needle-cases to balsa wood model boats. No one had asked the children to design these things; they just made them. Although much of this craft work could fit into the 'making' demands of the new subject, many primary school teachers felt completely at sea when it came to the designing, a problem that was compounded by the language in which the document was written, which did not describe anything familiar to the average primary school teacher, either on a personal or a professional level. Further, numbering 'Attainment Targets' as 1–5 suggested a strictly linear 'design process' which, despite the best efforts of the Design and Technology Association and the national research community ever since, has never gone away.

Primary teachers felt much happier with the 1995 revision of this document; it simply described designing and making as two separate attainment targets. Unfortunately, this implied two distinct outcomes: 'the design' and 'the product', which led to teachers expecting children to produce a drawing of their intended product before beginning any making.

The next revision came in 2004 and was divided into two sections: *Knowledge, skills and understanding* and *Breadth of Study*. By this time, international conferences had enabled academics (many of whom were also curriculum writers) from across the world to meet, share, discuss and agree on what design and technology was all about. This international community included influential figures from sub-Saharan Africa, curriculum writers from as far away as Southern Australia, academics from Canada, and researchers from all over Europe. The Breadth of Study reflected understandings across this national and international research community of what good primary design and technology education should consist of:

- investigating and evaluating a range of familiar products
- focused practical tasks that develop a range of techniques, skills, processes and knowledge
- design and make assignments using a range of materials, including food, items that can be put together to make products, and textiles.

The first of these quickly became known by the acronym 'IDEAs' ('Investigating, Disassembling and Evaluating Artefacts') but, not surprisingly, this led to misunderstanding that the sole purpose of examining the workings of existing products was to get ideas for designing a new product. Learning about railways, for instance, was not primarily in order to extend technological understanding about mechanical and organizational systems and celebrate a technological triumph of the Victorian age. The writers of the guidance for teaching religious education had wisely split their subject into 'learning about' and 'learning through'. The 'learning about' side of technology was sorely needed. It seemed to leave the appreciation of technological achievement for its own sake to history and geography. From an international perspective, Marc de Vries (Netherlands) commented on the almost complete absence of the wider impact of technology on society:

> It seems that whole curriculum is based on the role of pupils as designers, and not users of new products
>
> (de Vries 2016, p. 93)

Pause for thought

Is this a fair judgement? De Vries was commenting on the 2005 curriculum (the one dated 2016 is a second edition). Do his observations ring true with your observations in schools?

The distinction between 'Focused Practical Tasks' (FPTs) and 'Design and Make Assignments' (DMAs) is clearly illustrated in Figures 4.6–4.9 in Chapter 4 (contrast these with the finished products in this chapter). However, many schools did not seem to get the idea. There was much teaching that was claimed to be DMAs that looked a lot like FPTs with a product which lacked either user or purpose (often both). Rows of all-but-identical picture frames, purses, and so on stood in serried ranks along window sills and pinned to display boards. 'Design' had been watered down to choosing the colour or decoration on the finished object. Everything else was taught step-by-step, with little opportunity for pupil choice, decision-making or independent problem-solving. The problem was perceived to be: how could it all be fitted into the time available? If children were to investigate existing products (where did the teacher get these from?), do some practice tasks to learn appropriate skills and then apply them in designing and making their own product, it might take more than the 6–7 lessons available in a (half) term. Part of the problem was in misunderstanding the nature of the FPTs. Looking at Figures 4.6–4.9, you can see that these are simple practice pieces. The other part of the problem was that national curriculum documentation and guidance was framed in the words 'pupils shall be taught to …', which implied instruction, rather than a more open-ended 'pupils will be given opportunities to learn to …', which implies a rather different understanding of pedagogy.

The Nuffield Foundation (through a team led by David Barlex) produced a scheme of work based on the idea of 'small steps, big task' and the adage 'practice makes perfect'. These Nuffield schemes had much to commend them but they were overshadowed by the Qualifications and Curriculum Authority's (QCA) own schemes of work for all subjects, published in 2005 and sent out to all schools.

The Nuffield schemes of work can be accessed at https://www.stem.org.uk/elibrary/collection/2891.

QCA schemes of work can be accessed at http://www.thegrid.org.uk/ learning/dandt/ks1-2 /resources/qca.shtml

Although the QCA schemes of work only had the status of guidance, most schools adopted them, partly on the assumption that these had the status of a syllabus and partly in fear of Ofsted (The Office for Standards in Education) – safer to deliver the QCA schemes than risk failure through their own school's schemes not being good enough for the inspectorate. Despite dominating the landscape for 10 years, the QCA schemes of work are now only available through the national archives listed above, which includes pictures of the kinds of products made under this scheme.

The team that assembled the QCA scheme was charged with constructing projects that children could *make*. The design side was marginalized, to the chagrin of the team members themselves. Each lesson plan ended with assessment criteria, at three levels: lower, higher and average attainment. What these patently did not do was allow for a child to come up with a completely different solution to the design brief. Innovation was not high on the agenda; creativity had clipped wings. The wholesale uncritical adoption of the QCA scheme left many schools believing that they were adequately delivering the National Curriculum (often assuming the QCA schemes *were* the National Curriculum). The scheme remained without revisions until the introduction of the new National Curriculum in 2014. Although many schools had developed their practice and extended their ideas beyond the scheme, it formed teachers' core understanding of design and technology and made them unprepared for the 2014 National Curriculum.

What is the current state of primary design and technology education?

As well as providing post-inspection feedback to individual schools, Ofsted collates data and produces reports on the overall provision of schools in England by Key Stages and by subjects. In 2008, they issued a report on design and technology that was entitled *Education for a technologically advanced nation: Design and technology in schools 2004–07*. Excerpt 2.1 picks out some of the points they made regarding primary design and technology. Excerpt 2.2 is from the *Annual Report of Her Majesty's Chief Inspector of Education, Children's Services and Skills 2015/1* (available at www.gov.uk/government/publications).

> **Pause for thought**
>
> Read these two reports carefully and compare their content. What differences do you notice between the two reports? Which is the more positive? What changes might have occurred between the two reports? How fair do you believe these reports to be? Do they reflect what you have seen in schools?

> **EXCERPT 2.1: Ofsted Report 2008**
>
> Pupils in the primary schools visited enjoyed design and technology. They were often proud of their creativity and skills as they designed and made functioning products. They behaved well and worked sensibly and safely with tools and equipment. Pupils' achievement and progress across the full spectrum of design and technology were good in about a third of the primary schools visited, but no better than satisfactory in over two thirds. However, there was some evidence of a trend of improvement.
>
> In most of the primary schools in the survey, design and technology continued to be on the margins of the curriculum. Only a third of schools offered a provision which rose above the bare minimum to be judged satisfactory. This lack of attention to the subject is related to the understandable focus on English, mathematics and science, as well as to the difficulties schools perceive in teaching a subject which is a complex amalgam of a number of formerly separate subjects, and includes substantial technical content.
>
> At least two thirds of the primary schools … have not realised the potential of design and technology to help all learners become confident and capable members of a technologically advanced society.

> **EXCERPT 2.2: Ofsted Report 2016**
>
> Inspectors gathered evidence about design and technology (D&T) provision from 26 primary schools in 2016. The proportion of time pupils spend on the iterative design process, working creatively to solve relevant design problems, was typically very limited. Often the D&T projects were linked to a whole-school theme or topic. This resulted in a prevalence of projects that asked pupils to 'design' a model of a historical item such as a Tudor house, a Mayan headdress, Roman shields or pottery. Leaders and teachers described these as design projects when they were actually 'craft model making' activities, neither improving the pupils' historical knowledge nor their D&T expertise. Some projects linked to themes such as space and transport required pupils to design a space rocket, or a moon buggy. Such projects can inspire creativity and imagination. However, because the pupils were designing something they could not test the functionality of, they did not learn to refine and develop their first ideas into something that worked. Very little evidence was found of pupils having opportunities to apply knowledge of computing to programme, monitor or control their designs.
>
> Where school leaders had a better grasp of subject requirements, projects were focused on a useful, testable, age-appropriate context. Designing a vehicle became 'design a vehicle for teddy'. Designing a rocket involved designing a rocket that could propel something into the air and for which the success of the design could be tested. Several schools provided a range of examples of pupils designing for a purpose. These included designing vehicles to transport an egg safely and designing and constructing shelters.
>
> When planning to meet the 2014 D&T national curriculum requirements, leaders typically focused on the end-of-key-stage expectations to define what pupils should be taught, instead of just using these expectations as indicators of where children broadly might be in terms of their knowledge, understanding and skills. In other words, these schools worried about teaching to the end-point assessment before mapping out the curriculum coherently. As a result, the overall aims and purpose of the subject were overlooked or not considered rigorously.

In 2008, Ofsted praised the contribution of the QCA schemes of work in helping to raise standards, adding: 'The most effective schools have gone well beyond these schemes to develop their own interesting and well-structured projects, which are closely linked to a carefully planned curriculum.' However, just eight years later in 2016, it would seem that this progress had evaporated. Does it imply that schools are doing worse, or that schools were delivering the QCA scheme in an increasingly routine way, which had increasingly marginalized designing in order to insure their pupils completed a successful product? How valid is a report based on only 26 schools in claiming to represent the state of the whole nation's primary schools?

One of the Ofsted 2008 recommendations was that schools should

> consider how, in the long term, science, technology, engineering and mathematics research and development might be used to create modern design and technology

projects, with mathematical and scientific content, to enable schools to keep pace with technological advances.

This has been addressed nationally through the STEM initiative (Science, Technology, Engineering and Mathematics). Although much of the work has focused on secondary schools, there have also been useful developments for primary schools. The STEM website (https://www.stem.org.uk/) is extremely helpful. Not only can all government documentation relating to design and technology (and the other STEM subjects) be found there, but also ideas for teaching projects that make links across the subjects. Be careful, however; some of these are more 'applying science' than 'designing technology'. Also (and of concern for design and technology), the word 'technology' is used in its more limited sense of 'digital/computer technology'. Engineering is the STEM aspect that covers design and technology as the UK curriculum understands it. The STEM approach is more in line with the United States and countries that have followed their lead in technology curriculum development, which emphasizes mechanisms, structures and manufacturing industries. Food and textiles seem to have to sneak in by the back door if they are to become part of the STEM family.

Pause for thought

Read the final paragraph of Excerpt 2.2. again. What pressures on teachers' time and effort are impacting on their successful implementation of the new curriculum for design and technology? Is Ofsted being fair in expecting all schools to be delivering the full design and technology curriculum just two years after the introduction of a new curriculum for every primary school subject?

The writers of the 2014 National Curriculum for England for design and technology knew that many schools would need to make changes to practice in order to deliver the new curriculum, especially in relation to designing and to the requirements for knowledge and understanding of electrical control in Upper Key Stage 2. They wanted to raise aspirations and expectations, to fit pupils for the technological world of the future, not dumb down the subject into craft activities with no user, purpose, intellectual challenge or opportunity for creative problem-solving. They had agreed that since the previous national curriculum had lasted 10 years, the new one might last just as long or even longer and, given the speed of change in electronic and electronic products and their increased availability and suitability for primary school children, it would be a mistake not to take the opportunity to try to future-proof the design and technology curriculum.

What does the current National Curriculum require?

The National Curriculum for Design and Technology for England 2014 can be downloaded at https://www.gov.uk/government/uploads/system/uploads/attachment_data/file/239041/PRIMARY_national_curriculum_-_Design_and_technology.pdf

> **Pause for thought**
>
> Who would you expect a national curriculum to be written by? The Minister for Education? Bureaucrats? What role do educationalists play in curriculum writing?

The group that wrote the National Curriculum for England for design and technology (2014) consisted of educationalists and leaders of industry. The Design and Technology Association was instrumental in liaising with government ministers, convening the meeting and presenting the proposed curriculum document. The writing process was made easier by two major factors: first, the extent to which discussions had already been had between the association and key figures in the Department for Education and, second, the fact that among the educationalists in the writing group, many of us knew each other well through attendance at international conferences, previous government initiatives and Design and Technology Association committee meetings. The chairperson for primary education, Kay Stables, who had been part of that community since before the first national curriculum (she was a member of Kimbell's APU team), with a high profile nationally and internationally, was highly respected.

Following on from the publication of the curriculum, the Design and Technology Association and the Expert Subject Advisory Group (ESAG) for design and technology produced a series of documents to support schools. References to these will appear throughout the book.

> **Pause for thought**
>
> Read the National Curriculum for England for design and technology (2014) and
>
> - Notice the way it is structured;
> - Identify key words and key messages (especially in opening paragraphs);
> - Identify any words or terms you do not understand (see the glossary at the end of the Introduction to this book or consult a dictionary; I have found that many students do not know what 'iterative' means)
> - Focus on the section headed 'The purposes and aims of the study of design and technology'

The 'purposes and aims' statement says that in design and technology, pupils should be solving real-life design problems, engaging in thinking about the real needs and wants of a potential user, applying knowledge from other subject areas. They should be helped to become creative, innovators, risk-takers. Pupils should develop their own ideas and evaluate those of others as well as being able to reflect on the success of their own work. Through studying design and technology, pupils should become citizens with everyday practical skills, resourceful, innovative and enterprising, yet also capable of critiquing the impact of technology on daily life. One practical skill is absolutely specific: pupils should learn how to cook.

In the introductory paragraph to each Key Stage, you will find the word 'iterative', a word purposely chosen to underline the point that designing, making and evaluating are not three separate skills nor are they three consecutive parts of a linear process to be split across different lessons. Designing, making and evaluating are *one combined, iterative process*. Evaluation happens as soon as designing starts; designing continues until the last part of the product is complete; both designing and evaluating continue throughout the process of making. However, I have since discovered through asking many groups of students that, unfortunately, they do not know what 'iterative' means. I then ask 'What do you do when you re-iterate a point?' and they can answer 'You go back over it.' Exactly. This is what was meant by putting the word in the document; designing, making and evaluating are an iterative, cyclic process.

The problem remains, of course, that many readers skip straight over this essential explanatory paragraph and see design, make and evaluate listed separately and misinterpret this to imply a three-stage process in which children draw ideas, make something and then write about it afterwards – a misunderstanding the national design and technology community has been fighting for the last 25 years. The separate listing of these three skills is necessary to explain what they mean, not to specify the order in which they should take place.

Look at the sections on technical knowledge in each key stage, especially Key Stage 2. These focus on structures, mechanisms and control technology, highlighting the links with science and with computing. This is a curriculum written with the future in mind. The previous National Curriculum lasted 10 years. This one might last that long too, and so it could not become out of date within a few years. The rapid growth of computer power and availability meant that this needed to be written into the specifications of the technical knowledge required for design and technology for the future.

Food has been given a separate section at the end of the National Curriculum for England for design and technology (2014). This is a reflection of the government's concern to ensure children learn about the importance of a healthy diet and learn to feed themselves well, so that it could be separated out from the rest of the design and technology curriculum. Bodies such as the British Nutritional Foundation and the Food Standards Agency contributed this part of the curriculum, based on their framework of core competences.

> **Pause for thought**
>
> Download and read the British Nutritional Foundation framework (see Recommended Reading list at the end of the chapter for the link to the web page).
>
> How does this framework of competences sit with the ethos of the purposes and aims of the design and technology curriculum?

These competences were not written to form part of a national curriculum for design and technology. The competences are based on principles of healthy living, and teaching children to prepare and enjoy good food are sound principles and should form the foundation of the knowledge and skills needed for food technology. However, as you read through the competences, you will notice that they are heavily knowledge-based. The words 'know', 'understand', 'be aware of' dominate. There is little about designing and choices are related to making the 'right' choice. The competences do not talk about the aesthetics of food; how to make it appealing in smell, taste, appearance or what the food industry calls 'mouth feel'. They do not promote experimentation with different proportions or types of ingredients (e.g. different kinds of flour for bread-making) nor a personal response to a range of potential ingredients in order to design a food product. Although the competences talk about the hygiene and safety aspects of food preparation, it has been omitted from the National Curriculum.

> **Pause for thought**
>
> Owen-Jackson, G. and Rutland, M. (2016) wrote a paper discussing the history and development of food technology in secondary schools (see Recommended Reading list at the end of the chapter for the link to this article). What parallels can you see with learning about food and cookery in primary education?

Cross-curricular links

> **Pause for thought**
>
> Think about your observations in primary schools:
>
> - To what extent is design and technology incorporated into wider cross-curriculum topics? Does this enhance children's learning or can some of the important aims of the subject get lost in the process?
> - Where design and technology is taught as a more separate subject, what other curriculum areas are drawn in and enable children to succeed in designing and making functional products?

By its very nature, design and technology is a subject that uses and applies knowledge skills and understandings from many disciplines. It is well placed to make meaningful connections between and across other curriculum subjects, by

- providing opportunities for talking, reading and writing in a range of genres,
- providing the practical application of mathematics,
- providing the real-world context for scientific concepts,
- giving life to historical and geographical knowledge.

In the National Curriculum for England, the programmes of study in all subjects specify that there is leeway to move some topics or areas of learning around within each Key Stage and even between Key Stages if teachers feel this is desirable. However, this needs to be carefully thought through or the balance of the whole curriculum may be disrupted. The links go in both directions: design and technology can contribute to the enhancement of other subjects as well as the knowledge, skills and understandings of other subjects can inform design and technology. Whether planning for a single lesson, a scheme of work that will last a few weeks or a whole year plan for your class, you should always try to forge links across subjects. This also enables recognition of the prior knowledge and skills that a teacher can assume to have been taught in another subject and/or year group.

The subjects are listed in the order in which they appear in the National Curriculum for England (2014) and all page references in this section refer to this document. Similar links can be made across the curriculum of other countries.

English

A list of all the cross-links with the English curriculum would take a chapter by itself. Provided here is a very brief list under the three main headings of speaking, reading and writing:

- Every design and technology project will include speaking and listening skills: explaining, presenting one's own viewpoint and listening to and considering those of others, weighing up options and being able to express opinions clearly and cogently, negotiating skills, communicating clearly through well-constructed speech.
- Reading skills are developed through research for ideas in print and online. Pupils' vocabulary and decoding skills are stretched as they come up against technical vocabulary and the different genres of non-fiction and technical writing. They will encounter different ways of expressing information (charts, labelled diagrams, bullet points, etc.) and the clarity of these unpicked and discussed. Ensure that the non-fiction section of the class library includes a wide range of books about how things work, inventors and designers. Online resources should, of course, be used equally with those in print.

- Everything that is recorded will help in practising handwriting and spelling; it will also help in practising layout on a page, which is an important communication skill. Grammar will also be practised, for instance, when evaluating the work at the end of a project (those maligned modal verbs in Year 6: 'what we could have done better … .'). Describing to others what they have designed or made, whether orally or in written form, develops pupils' powers of description and develops the use of appropriate adjectives and adverbs in context.

Mathematics

The Purpose of Study statement that begins the Programme of Study for mathematics emphasizes the essential contribution of the subject to everyday life 'including science, technology and engineering'. (National Curriculum, p. 99). In view of this, teachers should ensure that mathematical understanding is enhanced by their pupils' engagement with technological problem-solving and product creation. Vice versa, the application of mathematical principles and the use of arithmetical calculations, measurements, the appreciation of space and shape, along with the understanding and use of charts, graphs and statistics in a practical application can enhance the pupils' deeper understanding of mathematics.

For example:

- ensure that the measuring skills needed for a design project have been covered recently in mathematics;
- use the design and technology project to review and apply the measuring skills that were previously taught in mathematics (perhaps a while ago).

The measurement strand of mathematics has strong implications for the level of accuracy that can be expected and applied to the making of products, especially in Years 5 and 6. However, while making sure you are not 'dumbing down' the measuring skills in design and technology, do not expect pupils of this age to be able to cut materials to 1mm level of accuracy. Most Year 6 pupils should be able to cut accurately along a straight line but curves will be more challenging and the longer the line the harder it is to maintain accurate cutting with scissors.

Science

The National Curriculum for Science specifies one of its three aims as being to ensure that all pupils 'are equipped with the scientific knowledge required to understand the uses and implications of science, today and for the future'. (p. 144). Although for most of human history the development of technology has not consciously involved the application of scientific principles, nowadays science is applied to industrial technology to ensure that products work effectively and production is economic. Children need to learn *why* a product will work, not simply be pleased that it might.

Note that there is no longer any study of forces and motion in Key Stage 1 (Table 2.1). The 'uses of everyday materials' in Year 2 comes very close to being learning about technology; it is most certainly applied science. Providing examples of 'people who have developed useful new materials', people who did so with users and a clear purpose in mind, is a good way to fit in some extra learning about technology.

In the Lower Key Stage 2 requirements (Table 2.2), there is scope for linking learning about food and cookery to the science curriculum. Work on plants could be linked to seasonality, farming and school garden design. The emphasis on nutrition in the animals theme creates a ready link to the healthy lifestyle messages of the cookery section of the design and technology curriculum. Interestingly, there is a clash between the healthy cookery requirements in the design and technology curriculum and the recommended activities for Year 4 studying States of Matter. Can you spot it? It would seem that pupils can still make chocolate crispy cakes – just call it science rather than design and technology!

The themes of light, sound, forces and magnets, and electricity have clear links to technological applications. The non-statutory notes for Year 4 even recommend a design and technology activity (designing ear-muffs) to extend the project on sound (ibid. p. 163).

In Upper Key Stage 2 (Table 2.3) there is a similar pattern, with a greater emphasis on biology than on the physical sciences. The Year 5 work on forces can readily be linked to work on mechanisms in design and technology. The study of electricity in Year 6 can be linked to control technology, as well as making links with the computing programme of study.

Table 2.1 Key Stage 1 Science

Year 1	Plants	Animals (including humans)	Everyday materials	Seasonal changes
Year 2	Plants	Animals (including humans)	Uses of everyday materials	Living things and their habitats

Table 2.2 Lower Key Stage 2 Science

Year 3	Plants	Animals (including humans)	Rocks	Light	Forces and magnets
Year 4	Living things and their habitats	Animals (including humans)	States of matter	Sound	Electricity

Table 2.3 Upper Key Stage 2 Science

| Year 5 | Living things and their habitats | Animals (including humans) | Properties and changes of materials | Earth and space | Forces |
| Year 6 | Living things and their habitats | Animals (including humans) | Evolution and inheritance | Light | Electricity |

Art and Design

Despite the bold claim with which the art and design curriculum begins (to 'embody some of the highest forms of human creativity' ibid., p. 176), the programme of study is described in the fewest number of words of any subject, which makes specific cross-subject links difficult. In fact, the first statement for Key Stage 1 ('to use a range of materials creatively to design and make products') could just as easily be applied to design and technology as to art.

It is unclear how a craft-maker (Key Stage 1) in art is different from a craft-maker in technology. Craft products can include furniture, ceramics, wooden bowls, hand-knitted garments, home textiles such as cushions, and even jams, honey and bread – in fact most of the products found in 'craft fairs' and 'artisan studios'. The inclusion of architects in the list in Key Stage 2 is not just misleading but, I'm sorry to say, simply wrong. An architect is designing a complex technological system with clear user, purpose, functionality and authenticity – not an art work. This does not at all help those struggling to clarify the difference between the two subjects.

Computing

The Purpose of Study statement for computing makes explicit links to design and technology, along with mathematics and science. Interestingly, the Subject Content uses the word 'technology' three times without qualifying it as being computing technology. The Programme of Study for computing is securely focused on programming and the use of digital technology. It makes specific mention of input and output in the second point under Key Stage 2 (ibid., p. 179), which provides scope to link this to Technical Knowledge at Key Stage 2 of the design and technology curriculum (ibid., p. 182).

A key use of digital technology is access to a very wide range of information on existing products which children can evaluate and adapt in creating their own designs. Some teachers may shun downloadable resources such as nets for vehicles, recipes for food technology, patterns for textile products and so on, as if everything a pupil does must come out of their own minds. Provided the pattern or recipe is going to be evaluated and adapted for a specific user and purpose, I see no problem in pupils searching for printable resources. For instance, if making vehicles from sheet resources such as card, downloading and printing a range of nets would be much quicker and provide a much wider range of shapes to choose from than asking pupils to achieve a vehicle body as a result of their own measuring and drawing.

The Design and Technology Association has published a guide to linking computing to design and technology, available at https://www.data.org.uk/resource-shop/primary/applying-computing-in-dt-at-ks2-and-ks3/

Although aimed at Key Stage 2/3, teachers of younger pupils will be able to adapt the guidance given here.

Geography

Both human and physical geography provide opportunities for links with design and technology. The study of seasons and weather patterns in Key Stage 1 (ibid., p. 185) can connect to the cooking section of the design and technology curriculum which specifies understanding seasonality in Key Stage 2. The geography curriculum's Locational Knowledge section includes land-use, which could incorporate agriculture, forestry and aquaculture as well as mineral resources. Through making links to geographical features and the distribution of resources, pupils can learn why different cultures develop and apply different kinds of technology to apparently similar problems or needs.

Under Place Knowledge in Key Stage 2, 'types of settlement and land use, economic activity including trade links, and the distribution of natural resources including energy, food, minerals and water' (ibid., p. 186), there are opportunities for learning about technology (houses, buildings and other structures, farming, fishing, communications including roads and transport systems, food and cooking, sources of materials and so on). Figure 2.1 shows two aspects of development of Tyneside: the bridges which enabled the distribution of coal and industrial products, and the Sage which has spearheaded the urban renewal after the industry departed. There was no bridge over the Tyne until the mid-nineteenth century when the two-level High Bridge was built, carrying both rail and vehicles, the one above the other. It is now one of the series of bridges linking Newcastle and Gateshead to the rest of the country, enabling their industrial development. Recently, the Sage has become a catalyst for urban renewal in Gateshead, along with the Angel of the North and the Baltic Centre. This stunning building is a technological masterpiece.

History

History provides the framework for understanding how our modern technological world developed in the way that it did. The history curriculum explicitly mentions technology at several points in the Subject Content for Key Stage 2. The story of

Figure 2.1 How technology has transformed landscape on Tyneside: (a) A view through the bridges of Newcastle-upon-Tyne from the Millennium Bridge; (b) The Sage, Gateshead

human development cannot be separated from our technological development; the interaction between our tools and our brains through our hands and our imaginations that made us evolve into the species that we are. However, teachers must be sure to avoid any suggestion that people in times and places other than our own were somehow inferior to us because they had not invented or used as many things. This is especially pertinent to a study of the Stone Age in Britain. Pupils should develop a sense of awe at the achievements of these people in the ancient past, especially in relation to World Heritage sites such as Stenness, the Ring of Brodgar, Scara Brae and Maes Howe in Orkney (see Figure 2.2). The study of these Neolithic cultures also helps to provide children in England a wider view of the cultural heritage of more northern parts of the UK.

Figure 2.2 Neolithic technology in Orkney: (a) The Standing Stones of Stenness; (b) Scara Brae Neolithic village

The local history study on the Key Stage 2 history curriculum should include the local agricultural, industrial or maritime heritage. A village school might look at the development of farming methods and machinery; an urban school may be able to visit an industrial heritage site; one near the coast may find docks for fisheries or merchant ships. Railways are mentioned in the geography curriculum, as are canals which kick-started the efficient transportation of materials and goods on which the Industrial Revolution thrived, now converted to heritage and holiday waterways (Figure 2.3).

Figure 2.3 Canals: (a) The Caledonian canal and the centre of Birmingham; (b) The canals kick-started the Industrial Revolution which created the world we live in today

Religious Education

The Curriculum Framework for Religious Education in England (2013) does not have the legislative status of the National Curriculum but its recommendations are followed in the majority of schools. There appears at first sight to be little connection between technology and religious education beyond an examination of buildings such as churches and synagogues. However, Howe, Davies and Ritchie (2001) asserted that the admiration of finely crafted artefacts has a spiritual aspect. By this, they mean the awe one feels on walking into a huge space such as a cathedral or major theatre (the Sage at Gateshead, for instance), the admiration for fine craftsmanship when looking at Saxon jewellery, medieval illuminated manuscripts, fine furniture, and so on. They also include the 'wow' of admiration that pupils offer in praise to each other and the glow of pride at receiving such accolade, claiming that feeling this glow enables the individual to reciprocate and appreciate what is admirable in the work of others. In their view, therefore, far from being dehumanizing, technology (or at least the appreciation of it) can stimulate emotional and spiritual well-being.

The standing stones at Stenness on Orkney (Figure 2.2, upper image) are a masterpiece of technological capability apart from serving a deeply religious function, as of course are all places of worship. When visiting places of worship, point out the technology as well as the religious function of the building.

Many objects that we now consider 'art', such as reliquaries, were originally intended as functional objects to encourage veneration and enable worship. Medieval English embroidery, for instance, was highly prized and copes, mitres and other ecclesiastical vestments were produced in quantity for the European church market. Questions about such an object concerning its purpose, function and user as well as the technical issues of how it was made help to make connections between children's own designing and making and that of adult craftspeople.

> **Pause for thought**
>
> Read Case Study 2.1 and record your own reactions to how Carla might put these stray thoughts together as a basis for a science/design and technology project which also incorporates geography, and possibly an off-site visit?

> **CASE STUDY 2.1**
>
> Carla is on placement in a Year 2 class in a suburban primary school. Her class teacher tells her she wants to extend the children's understanding of the properties of different materials that they began to discuss in 'Uses of Everyday Materials' in science the previous term and relate this to materials used for animal and human homes. 'I thought they could do that through design and technology' she said, 'and any other cross-curricular links you want to make.'
>
> As she is standing waiting for the bus, she notices bluetits flying in and out of a bush over the road.
>
> She gets on the bus and as the bus comes out onto the main road, she notices a pub roof being re-thatched to give it an olde-worlde look.
>
> She remembers a boating holiday on the Norfolk Broads, with all the reeds growing along the banks.
>
> Her mind does a leap to woven shelters (Aborigines? Somewhere in Africa?) and then to hedge-laying along the lanes near her aunt's house in Suffolk.
>
> She suddenly thinks: weaver birds? Weaver ants? (do such things exist, or am I going crazy, perhaps it was bees, not sure, was it with David Attenborough or that other man?). Certainly spiders. Spiders definitely, of course. Weaving? What could children weave? What could they look at? … . Baskets! Everyone all round the world makes and uses baskets? Who made the first baskets? Does anyone know?
>
> Oh, goodness, my stop! Got to get off the bus … . Ring the bell!

Carla decided she definitely wants to include some weaving with authentic materials, not paper or card. She has just two weeks in which to teach this but her class teacher says she can have three afternoons in each week, plus she would be welcome to make links with English if she can come up with some good ideas.

> ### Pause for thought
>
> Can you complete Carla's first attempt at a planning grid (Table 2.4)?
>
> - Look back at the Design and Technology Association's definition of design and technology in Chapter 1 to check that you are planning for authentic design and technology, not just a 'craft' activity.
> - Think carefully about the product of Carla's weaving activity – Who is it for? What is it for? What materials might she use that will make authentic links to her observations from the bus?
> - Carla has thought about linking science and geography to design and technology; this is probably enough. However, English and mathematics seep in everywhere. What specific links can be made to the English curriculum? Can Carla also make links to mathematics?

Table 2.4 A planning grid for cross-curricular work

	Science	Design and Technology	Geography
Week 1			
Week 2			

An international perspective

So far in this chapter, we have been focusing on the National Curriculum for England – but how does this compare to that of other countries?

In this final section of the chapter we shall look at four other curricula from three English-speaking regions across the world: New Zealand, Malta and South Africa that have overall similarities with our own. Many other countries include technology as part of their science curriculum and do not emphasize designing to the extent that we do in England.

> **Pause for thought**
>
> Look at the New Zealand National Curriculum for technology (available at http://nzcurriculum.tki.org.nz/The-New-Zealand-Curriculum/Technology) and click on the links to the 4 separate pages.
>
> How do the 'What is technology about?' and 'Why study technology?' sections compare to the English National Curriculum and to the viewpoints expressed so far in this book?
>
> You may also be interested to look at the detail of the curriculum on the other two tabs and compare that to your own country's curriculum.

New Zealand's perspective seems very similar to that of England, as does that of Malta, as shown by this statement that prefaces the curriculum:

> Design and Technology combines practical and technological skills with creative thinking to make useful products. Design and Technology education primarily concerns 'design and make' tasks, where learners work through a creative process. They typically generate, develop and communicate ideas for chosen products; plan how to put their ideas into practice; select appropriate tools, techniques, and materials; explore the qualities of materials; shape and combine materials and components; apply safety procedures; critically examine what they are doing; and on the basis of feedback, plan to improve their work. Their exploration of materials will include Resistant Materials, Electronics and Graphic Products. The 'design and make' process empowers learners, as they progress through the different cycles, to intervene creatively in the manufactured world, manage resources in an entrepreneurial manner and integrate knowledge across domains.
> (Ministry of Education & Employment, Malta 2012, p. 35)

South Africa's Technology Learning Area (available at http://www.education.gpg.gov.za/Document5/Documents/Intermediate%20Phase%20Technology.pdf) provides learners with opportunities to:

- learn by solving problems in creative ways;
- learn while using authentic contexts that are rooted in real situations outside the classroom;
- combine thinking and doing in a way that links abstract concepts to concrete understanding;
- carry out practical projects using a variety of technological skills – investigating, designing, making, evaluating, communicating – that suit different learning styles;
- use and engage with knowledge in a purposeful way;

- learn by dealing directly with inclusivity, human rights, social and environmental issues in their project work; use a variety of life skills in authentic contexts (e.g. decision-making, critical and creative thinking, cooperation, needs identification);
- create more positive attitudes, perceptions and aspirations towards technology-based careers.

The three interrelated Learning Outcomes in the Technology Learning Area are

- technological processes and skills;
- technological knowledge and understanding; and
- the interrelationship between technology, society and the environment.

The first two of these outcomes include a detailed list of digital technology and competences alongside designing and practical capability with tools and materials. Alongside this, however, and of special interest is the third Learning Outcome which aims to ensure that learners are aware of:

- indigenous technology and culture: changes in technology over time, indigenous solutions to problems, cultural influences;
- impacts of technology: how technology has benefited or been detrimental to society and the environment;
- biases created by technology: the influences of technology on values, attitudes and behaviours (e.g. around gender, race, ethics, religion and culture).

In other words, South Africa consciously and specifically values its peoples' time-honoured solutions to everyday situations and the values that underpin them, as well as aiming for its pupils to compete on the world stage of hi-tech innovation. The link to the full document can be found in the Recommended Reading list.

> **Pause for thought**
>
> Look at the diagram on p.9 of the South Australia Curriculum and Standards Authority (SACSA) Companion Document for design and technology (South Australia National Curriculum for design and technology):
> http://www.sacsa.sa.edu.au/ATT/%7BF51C47E3-B6F3-4765-83C3-0E27FF5DD952%7D/R-10_Design_&_Tech.pdf
> In what ways does this accord with the view of design and technology expressed in the English National Curriculum?

Summary

In this chapter, we have:

- Looked at the development of design and technology in England across the past few decades in order to understand the historical context of the current national curriculum document;
- Compared reports from Ofsted inspections in 2008 and 2016 to ascertain what lessons teachers should learn from these;
- Pointed out some of the significant features of the 2014 National Curriculum for design and technology. This discussion was brief because the rest of the book is an expansion of this topic;
- Glanced at the other curriculum subjects to see how connections can be made with design and technology in order to provide a coherent learning experience for pupils;
- Briefly considered some other national curricula that are similar to that of England.

In doing so, a coherent picture has been painted of the current position of the subject within the curriculum of the primary school. It is recognized that the difficulty that many teachers have had in quickly implementing this curriculum in their classroom (and the difficulty faced by senior management teams to support and encourage them in so doing) has been that the 2014 curriculum covered all the primary school subjects. Naturally, schools have needed to prioritize those subjects to which greatest weight is attached in the curriculum itself and by Ofsted inspections (i.e. English, mathematics and science).

Recommended reading

The National Curriculum for Design and Technology for England 2014 can be downloaded at https://www.gov.uk/government/uploads/system/uploads/attachment_data/file/239041/PRIMARY_national_curriculum_-_Design_and_technology.pdf

The British Nutritional Foundation Framework of Core Competencies is available at https://www.nutrition.org.uk/foodinschools/competences/competences.html

Owen-Jackson, G. and Rutland, M. (2016). Food in the school curriculum in England: Its development from cookery to cookery, *Design and Technology Education: an International Journal*, 21(3), available at https://ojs.lboro.ac.uk/ojs/index.php/DATE/article/view/2159

South Australia Curriculum Standards and Accountability (2004), *South Australian Companion Document for Design and Technology*; The State of South Australia, Department of Education and Children's Services. Available at http://www.sacsa.sa.edu.au/ATT/%7BF51C47E3-B6F3-4765-83C3-0E27FF5DD952%7D/R-10_Design_&_Tech.pdf

Chapter 3
Design and Technology as an Irresistible Activity

Chapter objectives

In this chapter you will:

- Appreciate what makes design and technology so popular with children;
- Understand the nature of designing;
- Learn why food technology is a highly popular activity;
- Consider the impact on pupils if the teacher does not enjoy teaching the subject.

Introduction

Pupils relish the opportunity to develop their own ideas and see these turned into a working product. This gives them a sense of agency and of being in charge of their own learning. Their ideas are valued and they can see a tangible result to their actions. Many children learn best by doing and design and technology keys into their talent. For children who struggle with literacy skills, being able to demonstrate their capability through making things provides a much needed boost to their self-esteem.

Pupil enjoyment and satisfaction

Pupils enjoy high-quality design and technology because:

- it is a hands-on practical activity that develops kinetic and physical skills;
- they can see an immediate, tangible outcome to their effort which is self-validating;
- it allows them to make choices, develop their own ideas, try things out, evaluate their own actions;

- it values and uses skills developed in 'play' rather than 'work';
- it is intellectually challenging, juggling the boundaries between fantasy and reality, seeing if flights of fancy might work in reality;
- they are actively encouraged to work with their friends, sharing and adapting ideas together, rising to the challenge of making their own ideas public and available for scrutiny;
- their input is valued.

As Hampshire Education Authority's website says:

> Design is one of the most popular classroom experiences with children. It provides them with a range of immediate practical learning experiences and is invaluable as a source of creativity and breadth that children need if they are to thrive in schools and develop a love of learning. Design and technology provides one of the most compelling reasons for children to engage in extended writing and is the means by which many children can deepen and sustain their knowledge and understanding of science and mathematics. … Through working in design and technology children are able to develop a set of practical, organisational and technological skills which supports the development of personal resilience and independence, and enables them to achieve personal, creative fulfilment. Children learn to identify opportunities and solve practical problems through which they can intervene to improve the quality of life. For all children, D&T is the means through which they will develop the confidence and wherewithal to face up to the practical challenges in life. Design and technology is the only subject which gives all children a flavour of engineering which, for many, is a pathway to personal fulfilment and forms part of their preparation for adult life.
>
> http://www.hants.gov.uk/education/hias/designandtechnology

Most children enjoy design and technology because designing is essentially a process of playing with ideas, which can be happening just in their own heads or developed through interaction with others, through drawing or using construction kits, through experimenting with materials or techniques, through evaluating, changing, making new decisions on the hoof. Children with rich fantasy lives make good designers; they have considerable practice at creating a logical system within an imaginatively constructed world. Designing things is fun, challenging, social, rewarding when it works, frustrating when it does not, which is all part of learning to deal with the real world as it is rather than how you might like it to be.

Developing a successful product requires:

- oral skills of describing, persuading, negotiating;
- listening skills to take on board ideas, suggestions and critique offered by others;
- reading and writing skills to research, clarify and communicate ideas;
- mathematical skills of estimating and measuring;

- drawing skills to develop ideas ahead of making and to communicate these effectively to others;
- scientific understanding of how forces work on materials, components and ingredients;
- artistic skills to make it appealing to a user;
- social skills to work together, sharing difficulties and successes;
- ethical, moral, cultural and possibly religious issues to be considered;
- the humility to accept the limitations of your own capabilities – but also pride in a successful product and a job well done.

Designing technology is multifaceted, drawing in knowledge, skills and understandings from a range of disciplines. In turn, its insights and challenges both enhance and question the way in which these other disciplines are applied in our daily lives.

Teachers rightly slow down children's design thinking and ask them to draw some ideas before grabbing materials so that hasty, ill-considered choices are not made. Rushing into the making may cause children to make decisions they may regret further down the line. Younger children will frequently make just one drawing that looks like the object they have been asked to make. They are probably using the drawing to clarify to themselves what the teacher has asked them to do and what their product idea might look like. This is a valid first step in learning to use drawing to aid designing. Older children can use drawing and model-making to develop their ideas before making a final product.

However, teachers need to think carefully about the role of drawing within any project – and vary it. Pupils do not always need to go through a full process of sketching initial ideas, deciding which they will make, then drawing it again neatly with labels and a materials list. Doing this for every project is going to become very restrictive.

> **Pause for thought**
>
> How have you seen pupils using drawing for designing in schools? Do pupils get any satisfaction from the process or do they really just want to get on with the making? How could you explain to your pupils the value of drawing ideas before beginning making?

The iterative nature of designing

There is no single authenticated and recommended way to go about designing things, like some sort of mathematical algorithm. The term 'the design process', unfortunately, suggests that following 'it' will lead to a successful design and hence to a successful product. The idea that there is such a simple, linear process came from the desire to see design as scientific. Hence the term 'design science' from the days when it was believed that science was the source of all knowledge and that all other forms of knowledge should work like science. Such 'scientific principles' were applied to manufacturing and resulted in the factory system with the division of labour and processes into small units that trained operatives could perform far more quickly by machine than could skilled craftsmen with hand tools. Henry Ford revolutionized the production and affordability of cars in the early twentieth century in this way. It was seen as the way of progress towards a brave new world (ignoring the mass-production of slaughter in 1914–18) and the assumption was that what was good enough for the production line must also be good enough for the design office. Close structuring of the 'research and development' process led, inexorably, to a situation in which designers were so constrained that they struggled to come up with good ideas.

But this was the world of industrial design, not of design-and-make. The world of design-and-make is that of the craftsperson or small-scale manufacture. The world of design-and-make is far less formal, formalized or formulaic. Its hands-on nature is far more akin to how children design and make things and how ordinary people make design decisions in the course of their everyday lives. Case Study 3.1 provides an example of everyday designing, and note how much talking Sanjit is doing. This is typical of designers and designing. In fact, talk and discussion is the primary means of developing and communicating designing ideas. How much of Sanjit's design process rings true in the kind of ordinary design decisions you make, perhaps in deciding what you'll wear for a special evening out or how you will redecorate a room?

CASE STUDY 3.1

Sanjit is inviting her boyfriend's mother to dinner. She wants to impress her with her cookery skills. She has some ideas but is not sure the starter will work. She rings her Mum who agrees to try it out on her Dad. Meanwhile, Sanjit thinks of an alternative idea but decides to wait until she hears back from Mum. Her best friend suggests a completely different main course to that which Sanjit had in mind. Which to try? She decides to have a go at making her friend's dish because she is pretty sure how her idea will turn out. She was part-way through cooking it when her Mum rang: a bit strong on the spices; good for starter, definitely not for main course. Sanjit tells her she's in the middle of doing the lamb dish her friend suggested. Her Mum's response: 'No, no, the spices are out of balance.' When Sanjit tried the lamb dish she liked its piquancy but decided to go with what her Mum had told her since it was likely that her boyfriend's Mum shared similar, more traditional tastes. She still wants to do her own tried-and-tested dish too, so decides to do both so that there is a choice. She is getting naan and accompaniments from the shop on the corner.

Design and Technology as an Irresistible Activity

> **Pause for thought**
>
> Download and read Cross (2001); reference and weblink are in the Recommended Reading list for this chapter.
>
> How do the points Cross makes about 'design science' relate to the points made so far in this chapter?
>
> Note: Cross's book 'Designerly Ways of Knowing' is well worth reading – and a 'must' for design and technology specialists.

Models of design processes

If we want our pupils to have wonderfully creative ideas and produce a worthwhile result, then it is important to understand some design theory. Otherwise we will be leading children by rote through a process we do not understand. Understanding how design processes work will enable the teacher to be more creative in his or her approach – and creative teaching stimulates creative learning.

> **Pause for thought**
>
> Look at Middleton's (2000) model of the route towards seeking a design solution (Figure 3.1) which captures the way ideas often develop. What is happening here? Imagine you were designing and making something – what is Middleton's diagram showing you?

What I see here is that, beginning at the left hand side of the diagram, the designer (adult or child) starts by realizing that there is more than one factor involved in solving this design problem (Middleton's 'problem zone'). One strand of design development goes smoothly (the route at the top of the diagram). Checks along the way (the double-ended arrows) convince the designer that all is well. However, parallel to that strand is a much more problematic path. There seem to be a few tangential routes and red herrings that occur, ideas that do not work, lead to cul-de-sacs or get rejected by

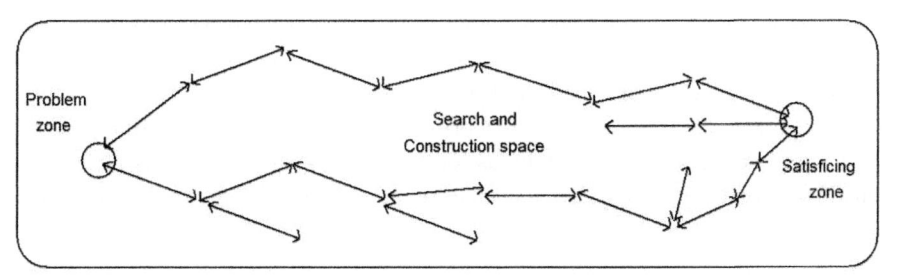

Figure 3.1 Middleton's model of seeking a design solution

the rest of the team. All this Middleton calls the 'Search and construction space', where ideas are developed and progress towards designing and making the product is happening. Note that this is a hands-on view of designing. This is *not* a model of 'design then make'; this is a holistic view of how designing happens for both adults and children.

At the right-hand end of the diagram, which represents the resolution of the design journey, is not a 'right answer' but what Middleton calls a 'satisficing zone' – a term he invented. What he means by this is that the solution satisfies the demands of the task or problem. It may be one of several possible solutions. It may be improved on later. It is a 'best fit' solution to the task in hand given the current state of knowledge, skill, time and resource constraints. Note that there is a short backward path pointing into the middle of the diagram. Has the designer done a final check back towards the original design brief – or have they realized there are things they have not considered and should have but constraints have prevented them from doing so? Perhaps the whole nature of the problem has suddenly become clear and new understanding has dawned now that they have developed the product. It could be any of these.

Middleton's 'satisficing zone' expresses the temporary nature of all technological progress, whether the designer is child or adult. For the child, there will be more refined skills and greater knowledge of handling materials which will pass on to the next project. The teacher looks at the product and assesses it as 'good' for the child's age or stage of development. When all their pupils' products are assembled, a whole range of solutions and different ideas will be seen, all of which satisfy the requirements of the design brief. This is equally true in adult designing. The design of technology never stands still. New products and ranges of products are constantly being developed to satisfy new and different needs and wants. This is part of the fascination of technological invention and development.

> ### Pause for thought
>
> Figure 3.2 shows Kimbell's (1984) model which expresses the complexity of designing. Choose one of the videos at http://www.bbc.co.uk/education/topics/zvrg87h/videos/1. To what extent does the making of the product demonstrate this principle of iteration: designing, making and evaluating all informing one another?

Some ten years later, Kimbell headed a team based at Goldsmiths College, University of London, to produce a report on young people's designing skills for the Assessment of Performance Unit (APU), which included the diagram shown in Figure 3.3 to express the interaction between mind and hand (Kimbell et al. 1991, p. 20). This diagram (often called the 'Christmas tree diagram' because of its overall shape) became one of the most famous 'design process' diagrams of its generation and formed part of the foundational understanding of designing within the design education community.

Figure 3.2 Kimbell's model of designing

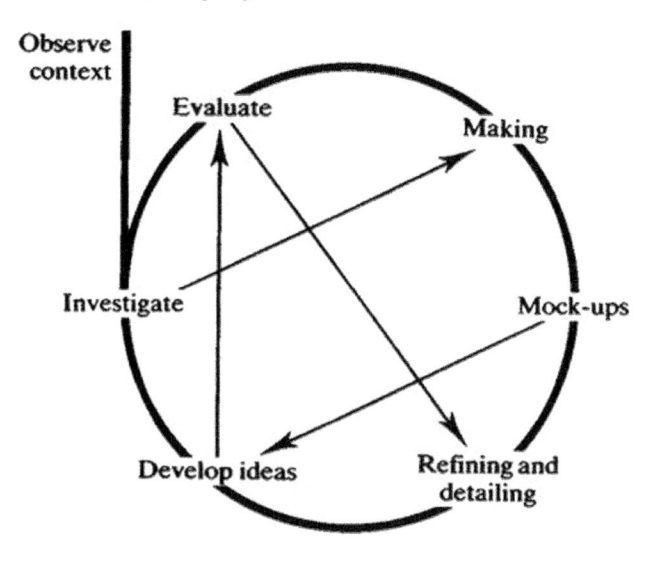

[Diagram: A circle with nodes labeled "Observe context", "Evaluate", "Making", "Investigate", "Mock-ups", "Develop ideas", "Refining and detailing", connected by arrows forming a star pattern inside the circle.]

Figure 3.3 Interaction between mind and hand: The 'Christmas tree' diagram, in Kimbell et al.'s APU report

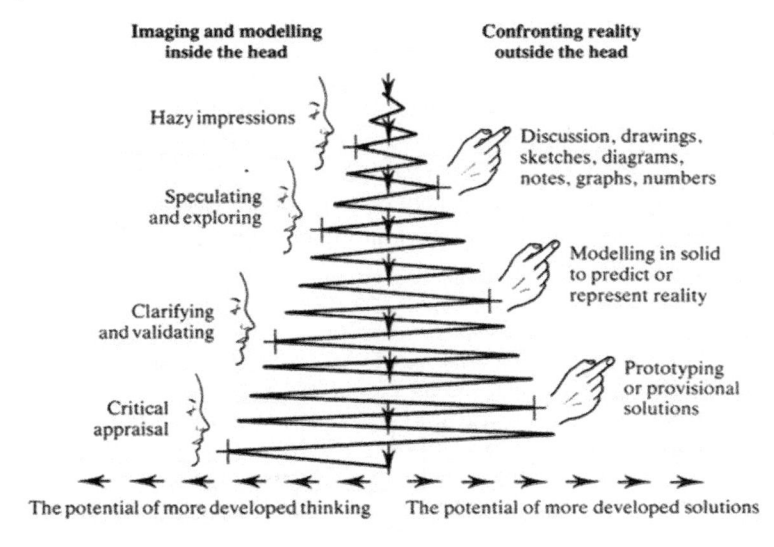

[Diagram: Two columns — "Imaging and modelling inside the head" (left) with stages: Hazy impressions, Speculating and exploring, Clarifying and validating, Critical appraisal; and "Confronting reality outside the head" (right) with stages: Discussion, drawings, sketches, diagrams, notes, graphs, numbers; Modelling in solid to predict or represent reality; Prototyping or provisional solutions. A zigzag pattern connects the two sides, widening downward. Arrows at bottom: "The potential of more developed thinking" (left) and "The potential of more developed solutions" (right).]

The skills that this APU report identified were:

- Generating design ideas
- Developing design ideas
- Communicating design ideas
- Making
- Evaluating

Figure 3.4 The dimensions of design capability

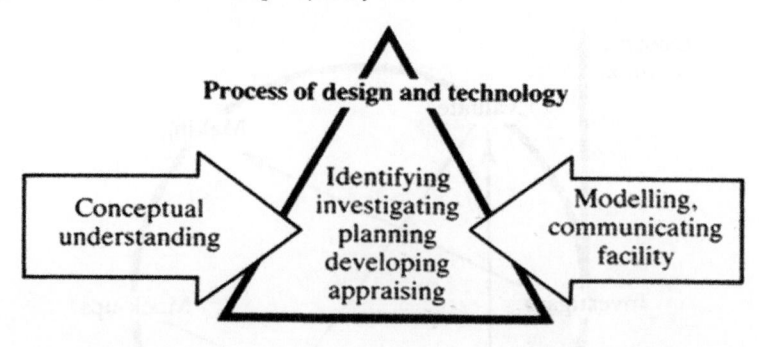

Process of design and technology

- Conceptual understanding
- Identifying investigating planning developing appraising
- Modelling, communicating facility

Figure 3.4 shows how the team saw the skills they had identified translated into the (then) new subject of design and technology (op cit. p. 29). They called these 'dimensions of capability' which suggest areas to explore rather than a straight line to follow.

> **Pause for thought**
>
> But does the list above suggest a linear process – and does it represent the order in which these processes happen? How would you plan for and assess these processes?

Rogers and Clare (1994) saw the analogy between Kolb's learning cycle and design processes and produced the model shown in Figure 3.5 with reflection as a central core.

Figure 3.5 Rogers and Clare's design spiral

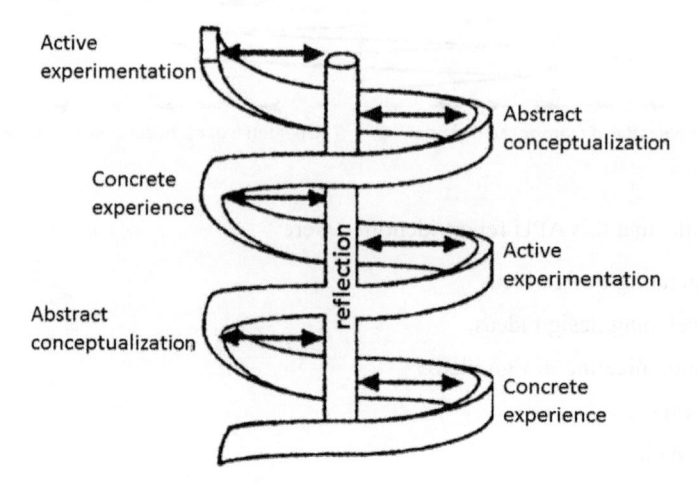

Pause for thought

When you next have the opportunity, sit and watch a small group of children working on a design and technology project and try to observe these skills in practice. Choose a moment when ideas are flowing, rather than the time when the children are nearing the completion of their work.

Case Study 3.2 provides a brief synopsis of such a moment and Figure 3.6 shows a drawing by another pupil exploring the same problem: A Year 2 class was asked to design a means for Frosty the Snowman to get across the lake between his house and Icy's shop now that the lake had started to thaw (using a boat was banned – they had to think of some other means!). A whole range of solutions including bridges, cable cars, rockets and tunnels was produced, all of which could satisfy the demands of the task and sit comfortably in Middleton's 'satisficing zone'.

CASE STUDY 3.2

Karl and Nathan were good friends. They were sitting next to each other, each drawing their own ideas. Karl looked across at Nathan's work and said: What you could do is … . (and started to draw on Nathan's paper)

Nathan said nothing, gave a sideways glance at what Karl had done and incorporated some of Karl's ideas into his own.

Later, as they began to make their product, Karl took the lead but Nathan quickly said:

> 'No, but when you looked at mine you said that wouldn't work. What we need to do is …'

However, once the class started making their ideas, both Karl and Nathan abandoned theirs and helped two other friends in making a very long tunnel.

It is interesting to note that Nathan interpreted Karl's input as 'saying that wouldn't work'. Karl did not actually make that judgement. He only suggested an idea that Nathan had not thought of himself. Presumably, Nathan had an idea in mind that Karl's suggestion overrode; perhaps that's the reason why he looked at Karl's paper to see his friend's train of thought that had prompted him to intervene.

Figure 3.6 shows Jason's imaginative rendering of Frosty's problem. Note the different shark species in the lake and the detail on Icy's vehicle (top left). Jason's solution is that Frosty stays where he is and Icy launches his all-purpose flying delivery vehicle loaded with all of Frosty's shopping. Jason is not simply designing a product, he is engaged in modelling the whole problem and its solution in a pictorial form of storytelling, which we can read. He was probably telling the whole story to his best friend Michael as he drew it. He was the only child in the class who

Figure 3.6 Frosty's problem and Icy's solution as worked out by Jason

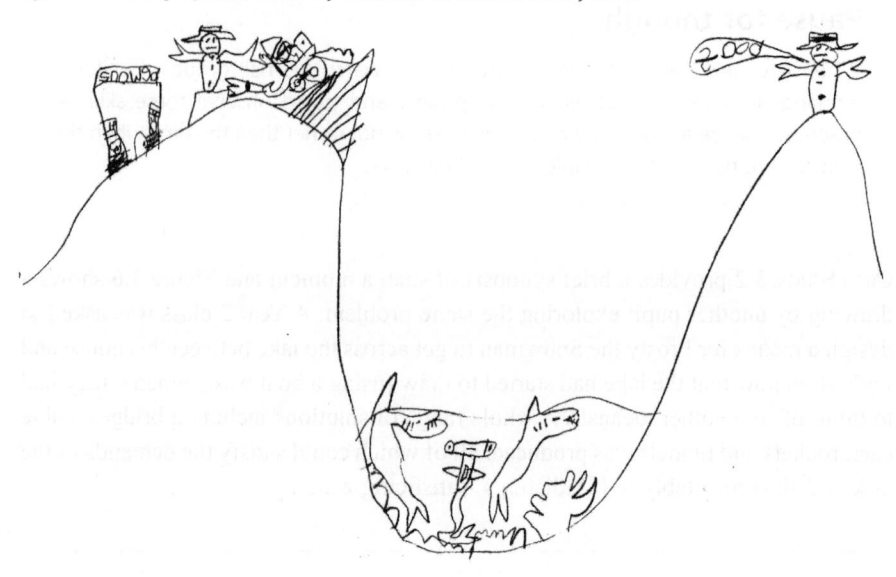

turned the problem completely around so that Icy provided the solution. This was real innovative thinking – the most creative solution in the whole class.

A child-friendly version of design process is available at http://www.childrensengineering.com/CEEDesignLoop2010.pdf

This is worth displaying and discussing in the classroom.

What is a creative solution to a technological challenge (and what is not)?

Pupils enjoy and are stimulated by challenges that allow them to be creative. Part of the appeal of design and technology is that it affords opportunity for pupils to act on their own ideas in a way that is more limited in some other subjects. It would be a shame, therefore, if the design brief provided little real challenge and limited scope for creativity.

> **Pause for thought**
>
> Read Case Study 3.3, an excerpt from an ITE lecturer's introduction to a seminar, designed to get the students thinking and talking. What is your reaction to the input and the two challenges by students? If possible, discuss these with a partner or in a small group.

CASE STUDY 3.3

Lecturer: 'For many years, the QCA schemes of work were followed in schools for most subjects including design and technology. Much of the content was laudable but its sheer existence encouraged teachers to repeat the same projects year on year and not to encourage their own or the children's creative thinking, especially since the lesson plans included a list of expected outcomes. This meant in practice that I could walk along school corridors and know which was the Year 2 class by its display of little "Joseph's cloaks" and Year 6 by the dangling slippers (and often there was only time for each child to make one slipper – don't get me started on that one …). Why on earth did the teachers not branch out. Footwear, not just slippers? That would have been so much more exciting. Think of all the possibilities! *(Tutor prances about as if on catwalk. Students titter as expected)* But the scheme specified slippers in order to develop sewing skills.

'Plus, many teachers had a linear view of designing so that children wasted time making drawings of things they could perfectly well make without drawing anything; or at the very start of a project, the children had to make drawings although they did not have enough knowledge of the materials or techniques to be able to use drawing effectively for modelling their developing ideas. So, although the QCA schemes gave teachers confidence, this was often at the expense of developing their own genuine expertise, understanding and creativity, with the knock-on effect that children's creativity suffered too and resulted in all those dreadful slippers with the only difference among them being the logo on the front.'

Challenge by student 1:

'But what is wrong with everyone having a successful product, even if they are all very similar? Is the emphasis on creativity not dispiriting to the child who finds having innovative ideas difficult? What happens about the products that do not work, even though a child has spent hours trying hard? Is it sufficient to say that a child has learnt a lot even if his or her product is not finished or falls apart? What about the child's self-esteem?'

Challenge by student 2:

'How many creative solutions are there to one problem? A slipper is a slipper, so there cannot be many different variations to that but isn't it the same with vehicles? They all need wheels and axles. Or food technology: the product has to be edible, surely, so they need to follow a recipe that works?'

Challenge by student 3:

'I agree that children's creativity is important but can they value their own effort and creativity above not producing something that works and looks good, especially if all their friends have done it? Would adults, even? I recently started going to pottery classes. I go along each week with an idea for something new. I enjoy it but I'm not planning to use my plates and bowls. I don't really value my learning curve, I just compare my poor products against those made by others who have been producing similar things for years.'

The tutor, of course, is being deliberately provocative and has succeeded in getting substantial and thoughtful reactions from the students, for which she commends them. In her summary, she comments that a balance is needed. Some design and technology projects clearly demand a high level of uniformity (agreeing with student 2 regarding the food) and some projects provide for a far greater variation of form of finished products than others. Within design and technology, *a creative solution needs to be a valid solution*. There may be a range of solutions clustered in Middleton's satisficing zone (Figure 3.1) but they all have to be satisficing. They have to fulfil the design brief. If a solution addresses some other problem or situation, that might have value in its own right, but it is not a solution to the design criteria as specified. In response to student 3's reference to her pottery, the lecturer comments on the difference between children's expectations and those of adults in that children are rarely expecting their products to really work. This willingness to accept an approximation of reality is part of the playful mind-set of childhood. We need to bear this in mind if we set the bar too high on the functionality of design and technology products.

But when do they draw their ideas?

My usual response to this question is: 'whenever they like from about 8 years up'. Which is not, of course, the answer that was wanted.

Pause for thought

In Case Study 3.4, Eleanor and Marissa are two mature students on a part-time ITE course. Both are teaching assistants; Eleanor works in Year 1 and Marissa in Year 4. They are discussing the place of drawing within design and technology lessons. Identify the issues each of these students raises and how these relate to drawing designs.

CASE STUDY 3.4

Eleanor: Oh, ours don't need to draw what they're going to make.

Marissa: But yours are much younger than my class. In mine, they have to draw it first.

Eleanor: Can they change it afterwards?

Marissa: No.

Eleanor: What if it doesn't work? *(Marissa shrugs)* My class can just go and choose whatever they want to make it with and if it doesn't come out how they thought, how they imagined, then *(she shrugs)* that's OK.

> *Marissa:* But how does that relate to planning anything.. to .. errm ... design brief and all that? Do you do cooking with them?
>
> *Eleanor:* Oh Yes.
>
> *Marissa:* And you follow recipes, right? They don't just mess about and do their own thing *then*, do they?
>
> *Eleanor:* Mmm. I think food's a bit different. Maybe, like you say, yours are much older ... .
>
> *Marissa:* But d&t is d&t whatever age, surely? I mean, what they make has to work, doesn't it?
>
> *Eleanor:* Well they pretend it does.
>
> *Marissa:* What about user and function?
>
> *Eleanor:* Well, it might be for a teddy or a story character, like designing a coach for Cinderella, but it wouldn't really *work*. But, like, do all the things your class make really work? Would their Mums actually use the bags they make?

Although in many schools it seems to have become part of the ritual of design and technology lessons, there is no requirement in the national curriculum that pupils should draw their ideas for every project. Indeed, for many projects, it would be more sensible if pupils were able to develop their skills with the materials or tools before they made design decisions about what they will make.

Pause for thought

How would you feel if you were asked to design something you were going to make without first handling the tools or materials you were going to use – or even without being told what they would be? Would you really be able to generate sensible ideas or develop them if you were told to just 'draw some ideas'? How realistic would these be? Once you handled the materials, would you not want to start designing all over again?

This is why the Design and Technology Association promotes evaluating existing products and learning new techniques through focused practical tasks before engaging in designing and making assignments. Without looking at existing products and handling the materials or learning the techniques that can be used to work with them, it is impossible to come up with good ideas. Therefore, drawing (if it is included in the project) comes *after* the product evaluation and the focused practical tasks. The innovative and amusing idea shown in Figure 3.7 came after rummaging in the recycled resources corner for materials and inspiration! Once this pupil had found the two plastic carrier bags, the desire to wear them was irresistible. Granting pupils permission to act spontaneously and valuing the result is the kind of creative pedagogy that should be at the heart of design and technology.

Figure 3.7 Why not Boots rather than Slippers?

Talking and drawing

Many pupils report that they enjoy design and technology because they can talk with their friends!

Discussion is the most powerful means of developing and communicating design ideas. In Key Stage 1, it is much more appropriate to ask children to have a discussion in order to generate design ideas than to ask them to use drawing. A real buzz can be felt in the room as children talk with a partner or in a small group about what they want to do. This discussion will not only help the flow of creative ideas but also keep pupils on-task. If someone is allowing their flight of fancy to go too far outside the design criteria, then a friend will probably put them right. After the initial buzz, the teacher can intervene, focus the class on the design brief and ask them to check that everyone in their group has produced ideas that satisfy it.

> ### Pause for thought
> What would you do next? Would you ask pupils to draw their idea? Or would you move them straight on into the making?

Often, teachers are concerned that young pupils will forget their ideas if they do not draw them. However, it could also be argued that while the creative juices are flowing, it would be better to move straight into making. The crucial question is: does it matter if pupils do not make the idea they originally generated whether by talk or drawing? Personally, I often find that by the time I have done some drawings,

I know what I do *not* want to do and dismiss ideas that would not work. Sometimes, therefore, the idea that I take forward into making is not one that appears on the paper. We must allow for pupils to do this too.

Design is not the process that precedes the making. Design is an iterative activity that begins with generating and evaluating ideas and does not stop until the product is declared finished. This iterative, ongoing designing is what makes the activity continue to be fun and engaging. If a detailed drawing is produced that solves all the problems, there can sometimes be little motivation to actually make the product. The excitement of solving a design problem and the joy of creativity has to be part of the whole process. Primary-aged children, especially the younger ones, need to engage in an evaluative making process that enables them to change and adapt their ideas as they go along. They may even produce a completely new idea part-way through the making process. If there is time for them to start again with their new idea, why not?

Examining and discussing existing artefacts and practising skills needed for making one's own can often promote the generation of design ideas. My colleague Eric Parkinson and I once did some staff development work in which teachers worked with small groups of Year 2 pupils. One of the sessions involved making finger puppets. The children were worried that they could not sew but by the time they had all practised some stitching on scrap felt, not only were they confident in their capabilities but they had been overheard saying such things as 'I'm going to make mine …' or 'Mine's going to have …' In other words, they were designing through discussion of the ideas that came into their heads as they completed the focused practical task of learning how to sew.

Food

Children love food! Any classroom activity that involves food is sure to be a winner.

Several initiatives across recent decades have been promoting cookery in school as a basic life skill. To qualify as food technology, food-related activities require some measure of design choice within the activity, not just adherence to standard recipes, as well as the development of children's understanding of the wider issues of food production and marketing.

Although the guidance for knowledge and understanding for work with food is listed separately, it is still part of design and technology, therefore the importance of pupils designing and making their own products still applies. In order for children to make healthy food choices, they need information. This not only includes such slogans as 'Five a Day' or the 'Eatwell Plate' diagram, but also how food is sourced, stored, processed and transported.

As well as cooking, consider growing your own. The Royal Horticultural Society's comprehensive website https://schoolgardening.rhs.org.uk has a wide range of information and projects for growing plants of all kinds, including building structures such as raised beds and poly-tunnels for the truly adventurous and committed. Ryton

Organic Gardens near Coventry is the home of Garden Organics and provides a range of useful information about growing flowers, fruit and vegetables organically in school grounds and in classrooms. This can be accessed through http://www.gardenorganic.org.uk/education.

There are many simple ideas that can be implemented to enhance growth of plants that reuse or recycle commonly available waste products:

- Cut the top off waxed card juice cartons to make plant pots (small or large) – or up-end them over dandelions to blanch the leaves and make them taste a lot less bitter;
- Reuse dessert pots for the same purposes;
- Mushroom trays make good seed trays; some meat trays are similarly deep;
- Cut the base from clear plastic drink bottles to make mini-greenhouses for tender plants;
- Make compost scoops from milk bottles;
- CDs/ DVDs strung on waste knitting yarn make good bird-scarers, as do scrunched up pieces of aluminium foil;
- Beans and peas can be grown up an old fishing net (for those who live near the sea).

Take a walk around local allotments (or, better, arrange to take your class there) and observe what people reuse and recycle. With permission, take some photographs to stimulate ideas back in the school garden or even a patch of ground outside your classroom. If it is all concrete and asphalt, consider getting some wood or stiff plastic and making your own planticrub. Many simple ideas which have stood the test of time can be applied to school gardens. Figure 3.8 shows plants growing in

Figure 3.8 Planticrubs

planticrubs (also spelt 'plantiecrub' or 'plantecrub') and the way Shetlanders protect young plants from the cold winds and driving rain. See https://myshetlandgarden.com/tag/planticrub/ for more information.

Figure 3.9 shows a full-sized greenhouse at South Nesting Primary School, Shetland. A smaller version could be built with the roof at child knee height – and it would not take as long to collect the bottles. Can you imagine the fun of making it!

The technology of food storage is another important topic, with links to science. Through combining scientific and technological knowledge, pupils can come to understand:

- how food can spoil if stored in the wrong conditions;
- the role of certain bacteria in spoilage;
- the difference between 'sell by' and 'best before' dates;
- how food can be preserved through refrigeration, freezing, drying, pickling, salting, pasteurization, boiling (including jam-making), traditional additives such as rennet (cheese), bacteria (yoghurt) or yeast (wine fermentation), modern chemical additives (most of which are harmless although some few have been associated with ill-health).

Integrating the science with the technology in this way provides a practical application of relevance to children's everyday lives. Key Stage 1 pupils can discuss and classify a range of foods according to their method of preservation. They will be interested to find out just how many ways have been devised to preserve milk – and how quickly unpasteurized milk spoils. It may be possible in country areas to obtain fresh, unpasteurized cow's, sheep's or goat's milk for experimentation.

Cottage cheese can readily be made in the classroom. Pasteurized full-fat milk should be heated to about 40 degrees Centigrade (it can be heated a little above this and allowed to cool). Approximately 15 ml of acid, either lemon juice or white

Figure 3.9 Greenhouse made from recycled plastic bottles

vinegar, should be added per pint of milk and slowly stirred. Curds will form. If this does not happen after about a minute, either add some more acid or warm the mix a little. Strain the curds from the whey. Mix in a little salt, herbs or chopped pineapple to taste. The whey makes a good mixing liquid for scones (use only bicarbonate of soda not baking powder). Warning: the cheese-making process smells 'like my baby brother's sick' as one Year 2 child so graphically put it and some children may not be keen to actually eat the product. However, this is exactly the process by which commercial cottage cheese is made.

The serving and presentation of food is also a technological issue because the plates, bowls and mugs, not to mention the knives, forks and spoons are all man-made items, as are the table and chairs. Although at first sight there seem to be few variations on the plate theme, designing a place setting for a three-armed alien or even for a character from a traditional tale or nursery rhyme might be fun. Humpty Dumpty's egg cup, perhaps? Use this idea as a take-home gift at the end of the spring term. It is something everyone can do, regardless of religious affiliation.

Fun to teach?

> **Pause for thought**
>
> This chapter has promoted the satisfaction and enjoyment that pupils get from design and technology. Are you looking forward to teaching it or do you have some concerns? Make a list of these and decide how you will address them.

Table 3.1 shows what some student-teachers said when asked:

Table 3.1 What I don't like about teaching design and technology

Alicia	I don't like the mess.
Erin	They get so noisy and then the naughty ones go wandering around the room and annoy the others.
Jane	I'm always afraid they'll cut themselves with a saw. I don't do blood!
Jadgit	I don't know anything about mechanisms.
Errol	I don't know how to sew!
Djou-yong	I've never been any good at anything practical. I gave up d&t at school as soon as I could.

I can sympathize; I have the same problem with music. I love listening to music and going to concerts but I cannot play an instrument or even sing in tune reliably. However, not being good at something yourself does not mean that you will not teach it well. It means that you understand when your pupils struggle.

Good organization is the answer to Alicia's problem. Having everything they need in a box or tray on their table should reduce the mess, movement and noise. For resources, tools and equipment that cannot (or should not) be on pupils' tables, think about the natural walkways around the room. You may decide to rearrange the pupil's tables so that potentially hazardous activities (such as Jane's saws) can be well away from other pupils working.

If you really know nothing about mechanisms or cannot sew, this is your opportunity to learn! You may decide to arrange for a teaching assistant to join your class for this session if they have these skills. Even the head-teacher may like to come and join you. School governors are often attached to specific Year Groups or to a specific cohort of pupils going up through the school. They enjoy coming into classrooms and enjoy being fully part of what is going on – much better than just sitting at the back of the room not being sure if they are allowed to get up and walk about.

Whoever you ask to support you in design and technology lessons, make sure they really understand what their role is and what your expectations of your pupils are. Some people seem to think that the aim of the game is for each child to have a perfect product, especially if it is something that is going home (e.g. Mother's Day gift). I remember glancing out of my room into the corridor to see how my helper was getting on only to see that the children were more or less just sitting there while she closely structured everything. She lined up the printing blocks; they just pressed them. She painted the glue; they just scattered the glitter. I was looking forward to my quirky collection of calendars but all I got was a whole set of identical products.

> **Pause for thought**
>
> How much enjoyment, satisfaction and sense of achievement did my Year 1 pupils get from this activity?
>
> Another thought: should you 'tidy up' children's products so that they look better (e.g. cut neatly around the edges)? To what extent is the finished effect their work?

Tessa's mirror project (Case Study 3.5) demonstrates the way in which an experienced teacher can key into children's own interests and create worthwhile learning experiences which extend their thinking and designing capabilities.

CASE STUDY 3.5: Tessa's Mirror Project

Tessa works with Year 1 and they have been looking at traditional tales in their literacy lessons. She has set up the role-play area as a room in a castle. At the end of the afternoon she observed some of the girls using a toy mirror and competing to be the 'fairest of them all'. She intervened to stop them squabbling and on the way home, she realized the potential of making mirrors and devised the following:

Science: What is reflection? What materials are reflective? Does the colour of the reflective surface make a difference? (Tessa was not too sure of this herself).

History / geography: Who invented mirrors and when? (Tessa had no idea of the answer to this, although she had seen Roman mirrors in a museum)

Maths: Size, shape

Art: Decorative features

Literacy: The children's knowledge of Snow White

But Tessa realized that above all this was a design and technology project and that all the other subjects were prequels to the designing and making of a mirror, which needed to be of a suitable size, decorative, reflective and so on. The mirror project could begin the next day with her providing some shiny spoons in the role-play area. The children could evaluate these and she could start a discussion about how they could improve on them / make their own … . Would this be a girls-only activity? How to get the boys on board? Could they design something else – ahh – what about Medusa, didn't Theseus defeat her by holding up a mirror? What would that one be like?

Pause for thought

Produce a plan for Tessa's mirror project that will:

- engage all the children in her class in an afternoon's creative work;
- does not demand that the children make detailed plans before making the mirror, a simple sketch of the shape which also shows how it will be held is sufficient;
- combines knowledge from all of the curriculum areas defined by Tessa, but focuses on the design and technology learning;
- relates to specific National Curriculum criteria for design and technology;
- demonstrates awareness of the health and safety issues that need to be considered.

Tessa decided to:

- Begin the afternoon by reminding the children of the story of Snow White and then read them a simplified version of Theseus and Medusa
- End the afternoon with a brief Powerpoint showing a range of mirrors, beginning with ancient Greek ones as a link back to the Theseus and Medusa story and ending with some photos of curved mirrors from piers and fairgrounds, just for fun, but also to make children think about how these were made.

Think about how you might encourage the children to consider:

- a different shape for the frame to that of the reflective surface (some ready cut shapes of different sizes, so that they could try these against each other?)
- the position of the handle (some trial pieces, ready cut, and some masking tape for ease of making changes, perhaps?)
- the colour of the reflective surface (does reality matter if it's going to be a magic mirror? In any case, they are probably going to be using shiny paper which is not really very reflective)

Tessa's mirror project has high validity in terms of the way in which the different subject areas work together to inform and enhance the different aspects of the design and technology project. Scientific investigative skills informed the children about reflections, which could then directly feed into their choice of material and colour. Mathematical knowledge about shape and the ability to estimate appropriate size were essential to creating a satisfying product. Artistic skills were used to make the product aesthetically appealing (even the Medusa mirror needed to look good or nobody would be attracted to look in it!). Knowledge of the literature was required for the children to create something that would satisfy the needs of the intended user, which would be different for the wicked witch and for Theseus.

Summary

We began this chapter celebrating the enjoyment that children find in design and technology lessons and ended with discussing why some teachers find it daunting. There seems so much pressure on time and on teachers to get their pupils to achieve targets in English and mathematics, some might argue that we cannot afford to put the effort into something so potentially messy and noisy and time-consuming that does not, currently, appear at the top of the list of national priorities. But many would respond: why deprive children of sheer enjoyment in their education? Do they not need a break from high-pressure, high-stakes learning?

It is subjects like design and technology that are providing the sense of well-being that needs to permeate the whole of children's education; the lungs of the curriculum, if you like, a bit like trees in cities.

However, it must be high-quality design and technology that the pupils receive and so we have:

- examined models of designing that underpin the national design and technology community's understanding of what designing *is*;
- focused on the role of drawing in design and technology and at what age it is realistic to ask pupils to use drawing to generate and develop their design ideas;
- indicated how children's enjoyment of food can be used to engage them in design and technology;
- considered the thorny question of what happens if the teacher does not feel confident in teaching the subject.

Recommended reading

Cross, N. (2001). Designerly ways of knowing: Design discipline versus design science. *Design Issues*, 17(3), pp. 49–55; available at http://oro.open.ac.uk/3281/1/Designerly-_DisciplinevScience.pdf

Chapter 4
Design and Technology as a Practical Activity

Chapter objectives

- To explain the kind of products that children will make in design and technology;
- To briefly outline the range of design and technology subject area expected to be covered in the primary school;
- To discuss food-related skills in some detail (food has its own separate section in the National Curriculum for England).

Introduction

As stressed in Chapter 1, design and technology is concerned with teaching children both how to design and how to make functional products, fit for purpose, that satisfy human needs and wants. Ideas for practical projects abound online and in books, often with cross-curricular links to create coherent learning opportunities. However, before delivering an off-the-shelf idea, refer back to national design and technology curriculum documentation to ensure that the learning requirements are being met, especially in terms of development of the children's own design ideas.

Teachers need to have the knowledge, skills and understanding to enable their pupils to turn their design ideas into reality and create a functional product made for a user and a purpose. The aim of this chapter is not to provide trainees or teachers with practical skills (that would be a whole book in itself!) but to outline the kind of activities in which pupils can engage. In doing so, they will develop skill and confidence in handling a range of tools, materials and equipment. It seemed sensible to leave these embedded in this chapter rather than artificially separate them out and list them again in Chapter 5.

> **Pause for thought**
>
> Read the following quotation from the National Association of Advisors and Inspectors for Design and Technology (NAAIDT). What do they believe are the essential characteristics of design and technology?
>
> NAAIDT believes that design and technology capability is best developed through being engaged in the purposeful practical activity of making things using a range of processes, equipment and materials. When engaged in design and technology activity, pupils should undertake work in contexts that are challenging, relevant and motivating. The emphasis on practical experience is central to design and technology to enable pupils to play a full and active role in a technological society and influence the quality of their environment.
>
> http://www.naaidt.org.uk/naaidt

What kind of products do pupils make in design and technology?

Technological products and solutions have the following characteristics:

A clear aim in mind: The purpose of a design and technology activity is to produce a solution to an identified need or want. This may be clearly focused, such as how to dig a well in a desert, or much more open-ended, such as fashion design – we all want to be stylish but we do not want to be all wearing the same clothes. Frequently we find science being applied to solve the technical problems and aesthetics being applied to satisfy our tastes and preferences in terms of styling. Pupils should be taught that, if possible, their products should be both functional and appealing.

Addressing the design criteria and the needs of the user: Not only must a product work but it must also work for the intended user. Much design and technology activity in primary schools involves paper and card, especially with younger children, which means that, strictly speaking, they are making models of products rather than products.

Producing a design idea that can actually be made with the materials provided: Avoid asking pupils to engage in glorious blue-skies thinking and then produce uninspiring materials that cannot do justice to their ideas. Children are willing to do a fair degree of pretending but they have their limits. Story characters and toys can have things made out of paper and card but real people need real things made from real materials.

Having ideas, trying things out, tinkering with them, comparing one's ideas with those of other people, doing a lot of talking. Avoid asking primary school pupils to perfect their ideas on paper (and call this drawing 'the design') which they then have to make, come what may. Adult designers do not work like this. It is a travesty of design theory to impose this on young children. The process of designing begins with vague and woolly ideas in the head, develops through the interaction between hand and brain, involves a great deal of evaluation along the way, and produces a satisfactory solution to the original design problem.

Developing skills in handling a range of materials, ingredients and components: To put their design ideas to the test and make something they believe will serve the intended purpose, children need to develop a range of knowledge and hand-skills across a range of materials, which involve cutting, shaping, forming and joining. The materials with which they need to engage can come in sheets, blocks, packets; can be soft, hard, squidgy, spongy, slippery; need to be combined, heated, cooled, fitted together, glued, left to dry overnight and so on.

Working safely: Correct ways of working need to be taught so that your pupils can work confidently without fear of either hurting themselves or others, or of damaging property or their surroundings.

Pause for thought

What practical work have you seen in schools that satisfy all (or most) of these criteria? Have you seen activities in design and technology that did not seem to have involved them all? Might they have been Focused Practical Tasks (FPTs) designed to teach children specific skills in preparation for a Design and Make Assignment (DMA)?

What counts as a product in design and technology?

A technological product is one that works well and satisfies a human need or want. It probably looks good too. When shopping, you automatically discard all those items that either do not work or are poorly finished. This principle needs to be applied by children making products in design and technology: the final result must be *fit for purpose as well as looking good*.

A model of something which works, but that does not perform the task of the original (e.g. a card model of a windmill) is, indeed, just that: a *model*. There is nothing wrong in making models. It is part of the exploration and design process. Sometimes, making a model is the final result of a design project and that is fine, as long as that is not the end point of every project. There are some things that children cannot make and a model will always be the end result. It is quite valid to ask pupils to make something in materials that they can cut, shape and join which replicates the real thing. One way around the problem is to ask them to design and make something for a story character, a historical figure, or a toy. They can then validly imagine that the character or toy can use the product and work within the parameters of its supposed needs. Getting the scale right can be challenging!

Figure 4.1 A large toy challenging scale using a construction kit

Figure 4.1 shows the seating arrangement of a fairground ride for a toy, using a construction kit to which the toy clearly does not belong. The challenge of providing this large toy has forced the consideration of scale, size, strength and stability of the structure as well as whether or not it will really work.

If we are going to assess children's work according to the Design and Technology Association's 'star diagram' (Fig. 1.3 in Chapter 1) then we need to make sure that the design brief we give them will enable them to achieve on all dimensions. It may not be possible to do so fully on every project as different projects may have different emphases but it is imperative that across a school year pupils have the opportunity to develop their capability in every dimension or they will be handicapped in tackling projects in the next year of their schooling. Imagine how frustrating it would be for secondary school teachers if pupils from some schools arrive with capabilities in every dimension and pupils from other schools do not.

> **Pause for thought**
>
> Consider each of the design briefs in Table.4.1. How well do each of them score on the Design and Technology Association's 'star diagram' (Fig. 1.3 in Chapter 1)? Which scores best (and why?). On which aspects do the others fall short?

Design and Technology as a Practical Activity

Table 4.1 Three design briefs: how well do they score on the 'star diagram'?

Lola, teaching in Year 1	Mark, teaching in Year 4	Sancha, teaching in Year 6
'Our class mascot, Sandy, needs some travel bags. When he comes to stay with each of you for the weekend or holidays, he will use your bag. The handles need to fit over his arm without dragging on the ground. It needs to be large enough for his plastic mac, hat and sunglasses – and the opening needs to be big enough to get them in and out. There are several fabrics to choose from and little pieces of them are in the tray on your tables to help you choose.'	'To help raise money for the new sports equipment, we will be making and selling biscuits. We need to think about the kinds of biscuits that will sell well. Today we will practise making the basic recipe and while we do that you need to think about how we can vary it and you can come up with all sorts of ideas for different shapes, decorations, flavours, and so on. While we are waiting for our practice biscuits to cook and cool, you can write and draw your ideas.'	'Today we will begin our wonderful windmill challenge. Working in pairs, you will use the internet to research different kinds of windmills. Then design your own windmill to be as interesting and imaginative as you can. Challenge: can you make it? Think about how big it will be, what you will make it out of, how the parts will be fixed together. How will the sails go round? Think about the look of the finished product: its colour and decoration – how will you achieve that?'

Let's look first at Mark's biscuit-making (Case Study 4.1):

CASE STUDY 4.1 Mark talking about the fundraising biscuits:

The whole school was involved in fundraising for new sports equipment inspired by the Olympics and my class wanted to make biscuits. We had a vote and that's what was most popular. I was a bit worried about it; it didn't seem to link very well to being healthy and the d&t NC Cookery. So I had to think how to get the most d&t out of it. Also, I thought – hang on, sugar gives you energy. It's not intrinsically bad, especially if you're doing a kind of sport …

Fiddling about drawing biscuits seemed pretty pointless so I was going to miss out that stage. We'd go straight into making. Then I realized they could do some drawing afterwards and it would be better that way because they'd have more idea. And they could talk about it while they were making. Users and purpose we'd got. So we could tick that box. Functionality – they had to sell! They were real biscuits, so authenticity's done. The one I was concerned about was the innovation since we were using a recipe but then they were all choosing their own shapes and flavours and stuff. So I actually decided to focus my assessment there. I wouldn't always. But with this one, most of the other points on the star were decided by me, for them, I mean, by the context. It would be mean to stand there at the table giving points to whose sold first and none to whose got left over.

> So when we'd finished and everyone's biscuits were on the plates, I got them to put the plates on the middle of their tables, so no one on the other tables would know whose biscuits they were, and then I sent them off to other tables and scored the biscuits on all the tables. They stood round each table and discussed the good points and I went round too. Then they all sat back down and we gave feedback. It was interesting because I was looking for innovation but actually the quirkiest ones that you might think of as innovative weren't automatically the ones that appealed most or looked like you'd want to eat them even. It made me really examine what I thought innovation is and that too much creativity isn't necessary to making a functional product. In fact it can get in the way.'

Mark raises a very important point at the end of his reflection. Is he right? Do functionality and innovation conflict? Actually, do we want the scores on these two points of the stars to *balance*? It is interesting how the action of assessing his pupils' products using the star diagram had made him rethink his own preconceptions about levels of creativity in relation to a product that needed to function and appeal to users in a marketplace. The veracity of his suspicions was confirmed on the day of the sale. He quickly realized that parents had given their children a set amount of money to spend and many were going round each class's stall to see what was there before deciding what kind of thing they would buy. The biscuits were popular but it was the decorated round ones that sold first, not his 'quirky' innovative shapes and colours. Flavour was irrelevant for sales. Only the oldest pupils asked what flavour they were (despite labels) but many of the younger ones said 'yuck' and put back the cheese-and-onions biscuits after one bite and one child got very upset and had to be given another biscuit free.

The moral of the story is: do not assume that scoring high on one arm of the star is going to make the whole product fit for purpose. The user might want something more conventional. On the other hand, thinking only of the users' preferences would hold back invention.

A good design needs to be balanced: functional but interesting enough to catch the attention of a potential user. It has to work well – but not necessarily just for the purpose in the mind of the designer; users are innovative too. The design decisions made by the maker of the product are key to its success and being able to balance functionality and innovation, appeal to a potential user and anticipate the way they might use it are all highly sophisticated skills. In one sense, therefore, 'design decisions' might be put at the centre, rather than on one of the arms of this star diagram. However, for the purpose for which the diagram was intended (to convey strongly to teachers the essential aspects of any authentic design and technology project and enable them to assess their pupil's work) it is a successful product!

Sancha's windmill project sounds exciting – but what is the purpose of the finished product and who is it for? It sounds as if some mechanical or electrical control is going to be added, so perhaps this is the purpose of the activity, to provide an authentic context for exploring mechanisms. This would be laudable and her pupils probably enjoyed the project and rose to the challenge, but she needed to be more explicit about user and purpose. 'To show a younger child how a windmill works' would have been adequate, provided it did.

Finally, Lola's travel bag for the class mascot. I have to say this one is fine – it was based on one of my research tasks! I like her personalization of the activity. The mascot is going to go and stay with each child for the weekend across the school year and will be taking the things it needs in the bag that child has made. This makes it quite clear that the bag has to really work. However, I discovered when researching this project with Year 1, they are more than happy to pretend it will work and make single-sided cut-outs of bags (see Case Study 6.1. in Chapter 6).

So, while I am happy with each of these projects for different reasons, the Viking boat shown in Figure 4.2 *falls a long way short of the requirements* for design and technology. It looks good; the colours are bright and appealing and its maker has found a suitable recycled container for the hull of the boat. However, the only way it could be justified as having a user and purpose is as a toy for a child learning about the Vikings – but even for this it fails. I suspect that neither user nor purpose were in the mind of its maker. Apply the star diagram to it and you soon begin to see why it is not a valid design and technology product:

- User? Purpose? Opportunity for creativity?
- Authenticity? Look at the size of the figurehead compared to the boat and how far back the sail is positioned, plus it is made from half a drinks bottle so it is not even the right shape – and did Vikings really have the oars sticking out of the centre of their shields?
- It probably floats, so it scores a tick on the functionality criterion but I'm afraid to say, that's all.

Figure 4.2 Viking boat: Looks nice but *not* design and technology

How can children's capabilities be developed across a wide range of media and techniques?

In order to be able to design and make products that really work, children need to have sufficient opportunity to learn appropriate practical skills in handling materials, tools and equipment. The Design and Technology Association has long recommended that this is done through Focused Practical Tasks, which are separate from the Design and Make Assignment. This second half of the chapter is organized under headings related to different areas of technology:

- Structures
- Mechanisms
- Electrical control
- Textiles
- Food

Look ahead at the photographs and identify which show Focused Practical Tasks and which illustrate Design and Make Assignments.

Structures

It could be argued this is the foundation of any design and technology work. Regardless of the materials and techniques used to make a product, if the whole thing collapses or falls apart, disappointment ensues. However, we will not be focusing here on the choice of strong-enough glue or stiff-enough card. This section is about teaching children how to make strong and stable structures from a range of materials by exploiting their properties; the practical application of scientific learning about material properties.

The Design and Technology Association separates learning about structures into two kinds:

- shell structures: made from sheet materials, such as paper, card, cardboard boxes and other recycled packaging; they may be made using nets or by cutting each section separately.
- frame structures: made from rigid struts, for example, art straws, lolly sticks, dowel. Sheet materials may then be used to cover or in-fill these structures.

Children need to know that triangles are the most rigid structures. Although construction kits appear to automatically lend themselves to making stable structures, many have very strong joining devices or specially shaped pieces, so the kit may not impart this knowledge. Kits that are sold as mathematical equipment can be used as an introduction to a lesson on structures. Both the examples shown in Figure 4.3 were made using a cool melt glue gun. This helps considerably with stability problems as it makes a secure fixing quickly.

Using recycled packaging as the basis for shell structures is quick and easy. Pupils can then concentrate on creating their product without having to worry about accurate measuring out, cutting and folding (Figure 4.4). The detail in the vehicle on the right would never have been possible within the time constraints if its builder had been required to make each of the sections from scratch from sheet cardboard.

Structures can also be made from mouldable materials such as clay, plastic modelling materials and plaster-impregnated cloth. As well as being useful for creating forms, plaster-impregnated cloth can be used to provide strength to structures

Figure 4.3 Stable frame structures

(a)

(b)

Figure 4.4 Shell structures: Vehicles made from recycled packaging

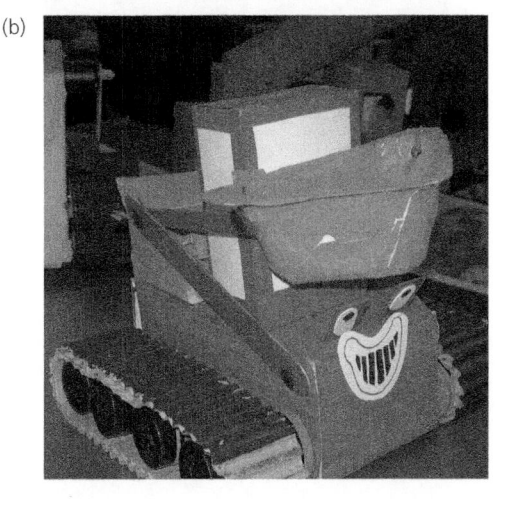

(a)

(b)

made from flimsy materials. For instance, it can be used to create three-dimensional corners by moulding it around the corner of a plastic box; ensure that any holes needed are made before the plaster sets.

Sculptures are clearly art objects whereas crockery, cooking pots and plant pots are technology because they are essentially functional. A vase is also a functional object since it needs to hold liquid but the aesthetics of the object may qualify it as art, so there is a crossover here. Plastic modelling materials can be used to learn techniques that will be utilized with clay in the final product. Pupils can be creative about the form of their product and simply copy in the clay quickly, efficiently and confidently. Air-drying clay dries out very quickly with handling, although having a bowl of water to dip hands into from time to time minimizes this. I have seen so many wrongly made coil pots, I have to comment on this:

- **Correct joining**: all the coils are smoothed out to make one complete sealed structure, as perfectly smooth inside and out as can be done by hand.
- **Incorrect joining**: the coils are not smoothed out. Leaving the coils unsmoothed means that there is minimal point of contact between each coil. The pot will quickly fall apart and even small gaps between the coils mean it will not hold water. Handles, especially, will come off in no time.

See Figure 4.5 for examples of this.

Clay can also be formed into functional objects through pressing into moulds. Shallow forms are better than steep-sided ones. The clay will shrink as it dries so it should be pressed inside the mould not formed round the outside (or it will crack as it dries). The mould must be lined with soft paper (e.g. paper towel) or cling film or

Figure 4.5 Coil pots: correct and incorrect joining. (a) Correct joining: My stoneware jug awaiting its handle (to be made and attached); (b) Incorrect joining: ITE student's basket (maybe it was art and so it did not matter that it was not functional)

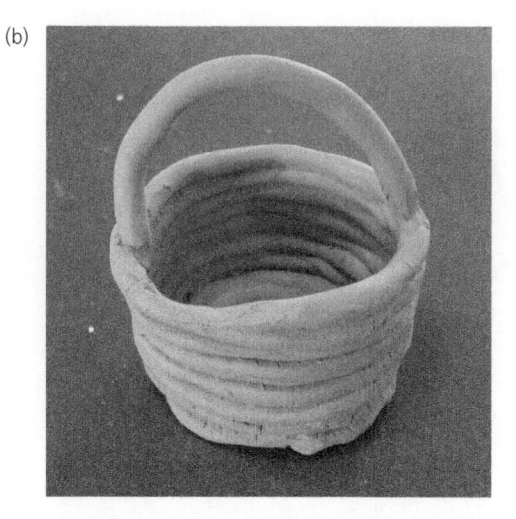

the clay will stick fast. Once dried, air-drying clay pots can be painted with a mixture of poster paint and PVA glue or painted with powder/block paint followed by PVA. Every part must be covered, including the base, as the clay will turn to powder from any exposed surface. So, decorate the pot excluding the base; let it dry; turn it over and paint the base with clear glue.

Mechanisms

Mechanisms make things move. It is the application of scientific principles of forces and motion, including push, pull, twist, turn, slide, roll, stop. This is achieved through the use of levers, wheels and cogs. More complex mechanisms (such as gears) are created as combinations of these three simple mechanisms (gears are cogged wheels, for instance). Hinges are simple levers, so any folded greetings card has a lever. However, not all folds are levers – only if they are designed to hinge. Pupils need to learn this technical vocabulary. Figures 4.6 and 4.7 show simple mechanisms suitable for pupils in Key Stage 1 that can be used in greetings cards. Avoid using these mechanisms just as moving pictures. It is harder to justify these as design and technology; *who will use them and for what purpose?*

To help your pupils to choose an appropriate mechanism for their design idea, it is useful to have some examples which they can then make and understand ahead of being asked to design a product (as shown in Figure 4.6, suitable for Key Stage 1, Figure 4.7, for Lower Key Stage 2, and Figures 4.8–4.9, for Upper Key Stage 2). Making practice pieces is recommended; these are the Focused Practical Task advocated by the Design and Technology Association.

Simple puppets can be made using levers, as shown in Figure 4.10. Note that it is surprisingly hard to get both legs and arms to move together. Tip: make slots in the limbs rather than holes; this allows a little more freedom of movement. Children tend to want to put the holes too near the edge, so you need to demonstrate correct placement. Insist that they use a hole punch to make the holes, which will then

Figure 4.6 A very simple mechanism suitable for Key Stage 1. Two strings are threaded through holes and attached one to each end of the picture. Pulling one (e.g. the left hand string) makes the figure move to the left and vice versa.

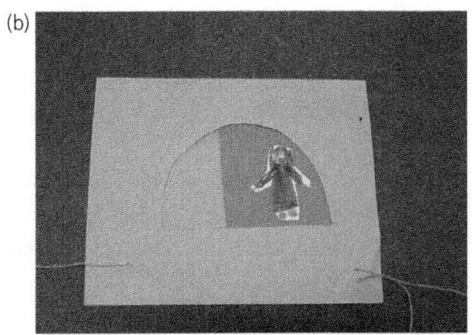

(a)   (b)

Figure 4.7 Hinge mechanisms for use in a greetings card. Accurate measuring, cutting and ability to understand reverse folding is needed. Year 2 pupils can achieve the straight-fold mechanism shown in the left hand picture; the right hand one would be more suitable for Year 4

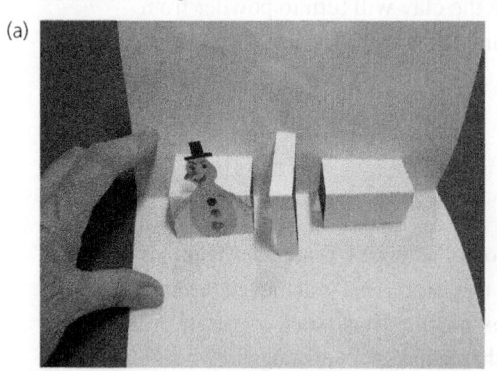

(a) (b)

Figure 4.8 This mechanism enables reverse motion. Pulling one end makes the other end extend and vice versa; pushing one end makes the other end contract.

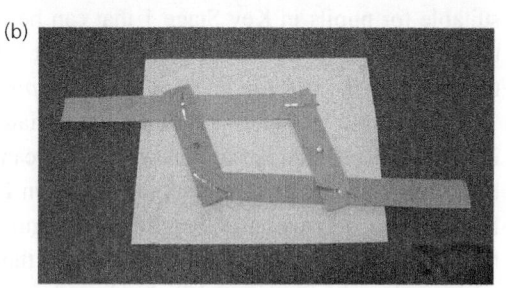

(a) (b)

be clean-sided and round, plus this is much safer than using the point of a pair of scissors. Reinforcing the holes with masking tape helps prevent tearing if they do make them a bit close to the edge of the card.

Learning about wheels and axles should include teaching children about the different arrangements of wheels and axles:

- Fixed wheel, rotating axle
- Rotating wheel, fixed axle
- Rotating wheel and axle

and a range of means by which axles can be attached to a chassis. It is worth making some samples, like those in Figure 4.12.

Younger pupils (Key Stage 1) will be happy to produce a vehicle with wheels that turn properly but older pupils can be given a challenge. Year 3–4 pupils can be asked to produce a vehicle with two different wheel-axle configurations. Year 5–6 can be asked to design a battery-powered vehicle using a small electric motor and pulley

Figure 4.9 A linear to rotary converter. The circle is attached by a split pin to the base board and the follower (the card strip) is attached to the edge of the circle (but not to the baseboard as well!). Pushing and pulling the follower will rotate the circle. The card across lower edge is called the limiter, which keeps the follower in line. The mechanism can also be used the other way around – turn the circle to get linear motion

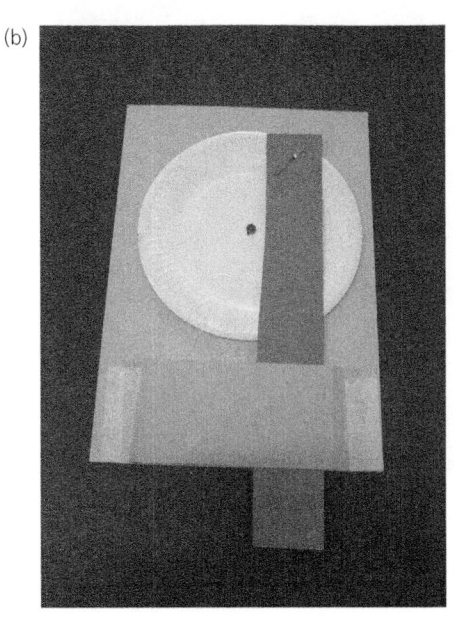

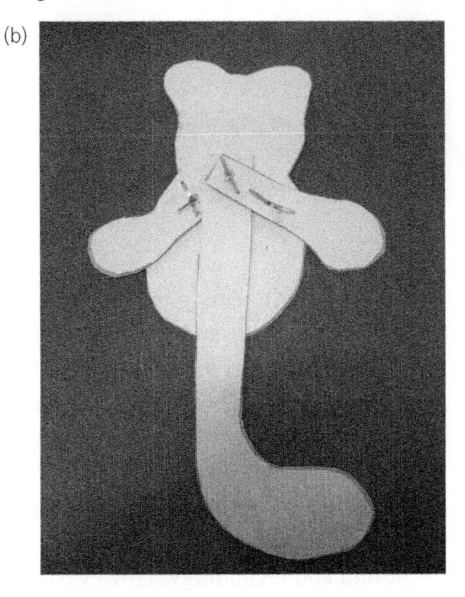

(a)   (b)

Figure 4.10 Puppets/toys employing levers: Arms moving

(a)   (b)

Figure 4.11 Puppets/toys employing levers: Arms and legs moving

(a)   (b)

Figure 4.12 Two examples of wheel attachments. Look carefully: which is which – fixed axle, rotating wheel; fixed wheel, rotating axle?

(a)   (b)

(elastic band). This progression in designing and making will build on previous knowledge, skills and understanding of the technological world – but children need to explore real examples of the different axle systems in order to understand their function and purpose (e.g. that an electric motor will turn the wheels if they are fixed to the axles rather than turning freely).

The National Curriculum for England for science (2014) places 'forces' in Year 5 which means that simpler understanding of the causes and effects of pushes and pulls, which were previously in Key Stage 1 science, are covered only in design and technology. However, this means that joyous racing of vehicles down slopes in Key Stage can now be enjoyed for its own sake without teachers feeling obliged to intervene and theorize. Whose coach gets Cinderella to the ball fastest, safest and with greatest style? The girls in the class can bring in their character dolls for the ride.

Many mechanisms are hidden inside the body of the product, making it difficult for pupils to immediately see how they are made. This is especially true of products involving cams and gears. A cam is essentially a non-circular fixed wheel. A gear is a wheel with teeth (cogs) that mesh with other teeth to enable controlled movement.

Both examples in Figure 4.13 were made under close supervision by confident and knowledgeable teachers. The Year 6 boy whose work is shown in the top picture attends The Meadows Residential School in Southborough, Kent, which caters to pupils in Key Stages 2–4. Pupils work in small groups under close supervision in the design and technology workshop, which contains a range of power tools not usually available to primary pupils. By substituting sheet materials such as thick card or rigid plastic for the wood (or even using recycled packaging), mainstream pupils could assemble this piece using cool melt glue guns.

The example in the lower picture in Figure 4.13 was made by a group of mixed Year 4 and Year 5 pupils in a mainstream Kent primary school that has the advantage of a dedicated design and technology room. The pupils had access to handsaws and bench vices set up on a dedicated table, closely supervised by the teacher. A teaching assistant supervised the use of the cool melt glue guns on the bench along one side of the room.

The carousel shown in Figure 4.14 employs gears: turn one cup and (with luck!) all the other cups will turn as well – usually just some do; the cardboard has a lot of friction in it. This carousel was made some years ago by ITE students in response to a design brief to imagine a fairground sited in a drab car park area in the city centre as part of the annual Canterbury Festival. The group of students who made this used

Figure 4.13 Cam mechanism made by Year 6 boy (left) and Year 4–5 group (right)

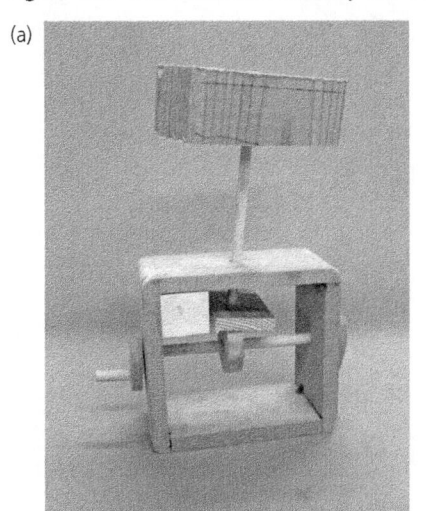

(a)

(b)

their experience of carousels and knowledge of gears to turn each of the pots which represent the cups of a 'Tea-cup' type ride.

Moving pictures are a good project for experimentation with pneumatics (see Figure 4.15) before asking pupils to design hydraulic systems such as a lift or swing bridge or to make a toy, like that shown in Figure 4.16.

Figure 4.14 Model of carousel ride using gears

Figure 4.15 Pneumatics used to create a moving picture

(a) (b)

Figure 4.16 A toy involving hydraulics part-way through construction. In this group project, the figures and other features were planned to all be connected to one another by syringes and plastic tubing, as can be seen at the front, so that as one was depressed by hand, another would spring up. A design problem occurred: the structure needed to be mounted on a much deeper box to allow space for the syringes and tubing to be fitted inside.

Electrical control

This is one of the areas that the writers of the 2014 National Curriculum for Design and Technology were very keen to promote. The previous National Curriculum had lasted ten years so, considering how computer technology had developed in that time, it was felt that pupils should come to understand and use electrical control in their design and technology projects.

Building electrical circuits has been included across the primary curriculum for some years, usually as part of science. I have even observed children in Early Years settings constructing simple circuits to make a buzzer work. There are obvious health and safety issues, such as putting batteries in mouths and breakage of fragile glass light bulbs. The latter can be avoided by using light emitting diodes ('LEDs') rather than bulbs. Batteries should be mounted in plastic holders. If children put these into their mouth they will get a slight tingle but not harm themselves. Packs of flexible wire with crocodile clips at each end are readily available, which facilitate joining parts of the circuit together. As we also noted regarding structures and mechanisms, design and technology is providing the context and application of scientific knowledge and understanding.

The most suitable electronic kit for primary schools is Crumble, available from Redfern Electronics, who provide full support for the kits via their website http://redfernelectronics.co.uk/crumble/.

Case Study 4.2 gives an account of an ITE student called Dane and his success with electrical control. Despite his disclaimer, he and his girlfriend had actually spent a lot of time experimenting and programming the kit so that he felt quite confident facing the class on Monday.

CASE STUDY 4.2

The school in which Dane was on his second school placement had just invested in a class pack of electrical control modules for their Upper Key Stage 2 pupils. Dane had expressed an interest in computer control and so was asked to teach the introductory lesson. He had never seen Crumble before, so he took the kit home, downloaded the programme and online guide and got to work on it. On Monday afternoon, he said to the class: 'This is a new kit. I've found out some of what it can do but I've not sussed it all out yet. So, it's going to be real fun today as you find out things it can do that I haven't. Then you can teach me!' They rose to the challenge; children love to be empowered in this genuine way. His mentor called by and commended him for the real buzz in the classroom. The design and technology subject leader was pleased it had all gone well – and even suggested that Dane teach her class the same lesson next week and she would act as his teaching assistant and learn how to use the kit!

Textiles

As mentioned above with regard to mouldable materials, there is often some confusion and concern as to whether textile work is art or design and technology. Again, think of use and function. You may have chosen your new coat for its fabric, styling and colour but if it does not keep you warm, it has failed in its purpose. Stand and watch people scurrying down any high street on a cold, wet and windy day and you will quickly notice how few have chosen their outerwear on its aesthetic appeal alone!

The fashion industry is heavily technological. New fabrics, new dyes, new way to cut cloth to create a certain look – all these are applications of materials science by a designer with a strong aesthetic sense and love of clothing. Work clothing, on the other hand, may need to be heat- or grease-resistant. Household fabrics, including curtains, carpets, bedding and towels, are not purely aesthetic. Their properties are also important – stain-resistant, insulating, absorbent and so on.

Children need to experience creating products that utilize the rich variety of fabrics and learn to:

- use adjectives such as 'waterproof' to describe the properties of a fabric, as well as soft, rough, smooth, shiny and so on to describe its look and feel; older pupils might even consider the hang and drape of fabrics;
- know that fabrics are made from natural sources such as cotton, wool, flax or bamboo, as well as man-made ones such as polyester, nylon, glass fibre, etc.
- recognize velvet, silk, leather, felt, and know that cheaper man-made substitutes are frequently used;
- know whether a fabric is woven, knitted or felted and understand something of the process.

They should also learn about the traditional fabrics of the UK such as Scottish tartan, Harris tweed, Fair Isle knitting and Shetland lace.

Textiles are not just fabrics, however. They include rope and string, straps and belts, and sails. All these can be found on a traditional sailing ship – so, when teaching about explorers on the high seas, include teaching about the materials the ships were made from. This present section deals only with how pupils can design and make a textile product.

Textile projects could include experimenting and learning:

- Cording (basis of rope and thread making);
- Felting;
- Creating knitted fabric: finger knitting, finger crochet, using a knitting dolly, plaiting, using a crochet hook to make chain stitch, knitting with needles;
- Creating woven fabric.

Fabrics can be prepared for making products by:

- Colouring: fabric crayons and paints, dip-dying, tie-dying, batik;
- Applying: other fabric either by gluing or sewing, thread (embroidery), beads (singly or in strings), buttons, zippers.

Applied objects such as buttons and zippers may be functional as well as decorative and may be applied during the production of the product rather than as preparation for making.

Instructions for batik can be found at http://www.dharmatrading.com/techniques/batik-instructions.html.

Figure 4.17 shows a method I observed being used in a workshop for visiting schoolchildren at a batik centre in Malaysia. The examples here were made in the UK following the Malaysian instructor's method.

The piece shown in Figure 4.17 is a first attempt. Pupils need to practice and evaluate their work so that they can see how careful they need to be when applying the wax to minimize drips. Bright or dark colours need to be chosen; in this example,

Figure 4.17 Batik method for children

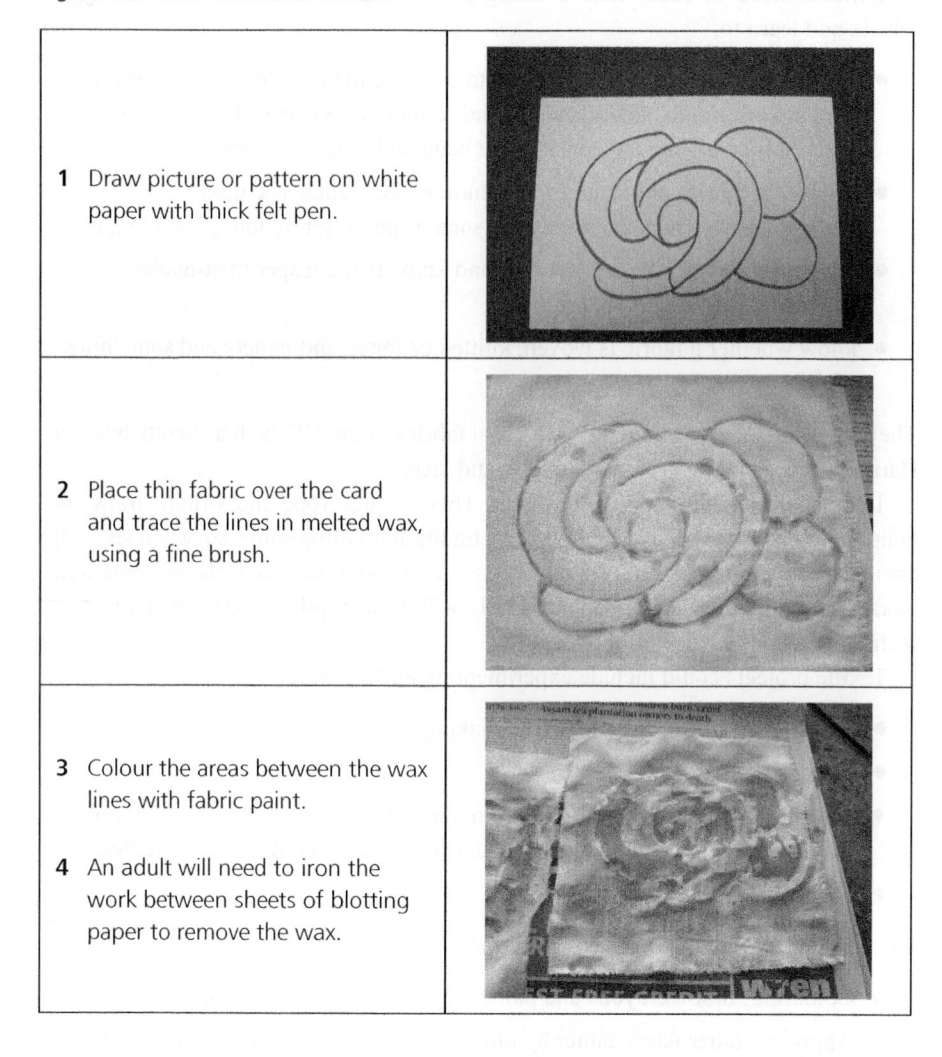

1 Draw picture or pattern on white paper with thick felt pen.	
2 Place thin fabric over the card and trace the lines in melted wax, using a fine brush.	
3 Colour the areas between the wax lines with fabric paint. 4 An adult will need to iron the work between sheets of blotting paper to remove the wax.	

the paler mauve does not stand out clearly. The fabric can be dipped into fabric dye and although this will just give a single colour, it is quicker than painting and would allow more time for several pieces to be made within one lesson. If done in thin fabric, the resultant pieces can be sewn onto firmer fabric to make into bags, cushion covers and so on. If you have fabric such as crepe or cheesecloth, this provides texture to the work.

When considering what our pupils might make from fabric that will satisfy human needs and wants, then they have the whole gamut of fabric wares to consider, including:

- bags,
- cushions,
- items that can be worn such as belts or cloaks or scarves,

- simple hand or finger puppets (see Figure 4.18),
- dolls' clothes (a waistcoat for an action figure?)
- or they can use textiles to add aesthetic appeal to a product constructed from another medium (as in the Easter Egg packaging also shown in Figure 4.18)

Do not neglect making fabric by felting, weaving or knitting. This is the best way for pupils to understand how different fabrics are made. They are then better able to identify the construction of commercially made fabrics and understand their properties and the reasons for their choice in product manufacture. The Year 6 girl in Figure 4.19 (overleaf) is exploring finger knitting for the first time.

Figure 4.18 Two examples of textile products by Year 5 pupils: a finger puppet and packaging for an Easter Egg

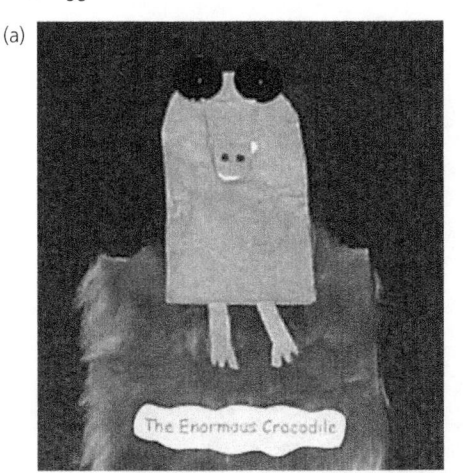

Drawing design ideas

Many teachers seem to have a fixation about children drawing everything before they are allowed to make anything. This is not helped by the number of templates available for 'design' process booklets that go 'first ideas', 'final choice', 'detailed drawing'. This is entirely appropriate for Upper Key Stage 2 pupils who are able to plan ahead and think through the processes needed to make the idea in their head. It also saves time in the long run through eliminating false starts and wasting materials. However, for younger pupils, especially in Key Stage 1, I would question the advisability of always adhering to the ritual.

My doctorate research was into Key Stage 1 pupils using drawing for designing. The findings demonstrated that before about age seven years, children can draw what they might like to make (to *generate* an idea) but they rarely use their drawing to *develop* their design ideas. They will draw a picture and may even annotate it

Figure 4.19 Finger knitting a belt

but the design development happens during making, not drawing. Year 1 children, especially, struggle to see the drawing as a planning tool for something they will be making. This convinced me that for such young children, asking them to draw design ideas was not worthwhile. They were asking me 'Why do we have to do this twice?' (i.e. once as a drawing and again as product). Asking pupils to engage in an activity of which they see no purpose is hardly likely to give them a good feeling about design and technology.

After analysing some 400 design drawings from children aged 4–8 years, I identified six different approaches:

- Picture (a picture of something somehow related to what they have been asked to do)
- Single draw (a single drawing of what they have been asked to make)
- Multi-draw (more than one drawing of the same idea)

- Multi-design (several different ideas recorded on the same sheet of paper)
- Progressive (one idea developed across several drawings)
- Interactive (several ideas that were combined and developed into a coherent drawing)

Hope (2005) shows examples of each category (see Recommended Reading list at the end of the chapter for weblink).

Although this list demonstrates progress in understanding and usage of drawing for designing, it became clear that Multi-design and Progressive drawings were different strategies chosen by the same children on different occasions. Their choice of strategy depended on whether they immediately had one strong idea which they developed (Progressive) or could imagine a range of possibilities (Multi-design) which they recorded with quick sketches and then chose one to make. Thus, the insistence on 'draw 3, choose 1' is inappropriate; 'draw as many or as few as you can think of in 10 minutes' would be far better.

Only a few of the children used their drawings interactively. In this category, I was looking for clear evidence of the child having assessed the drawings and recombined elements to create a new idea. For the average 8-year-old, using drawing to progress their design ideas was as far as they were capable of going. Many 8-year-olds' drawings showed some elements of progression, even the Multi-design ones.

The concept of 'ideas on a journey' became my metaphor for teaching designing, regardless of the medium they were using. Figure 4.20 shows an example of two Year 2 boys using plastic modelling clay and consumable resources to design a marble run to be made at a much larger scale with permanent fixings and more durable materials. However, these two boys did not make this idea. This was the first of several design

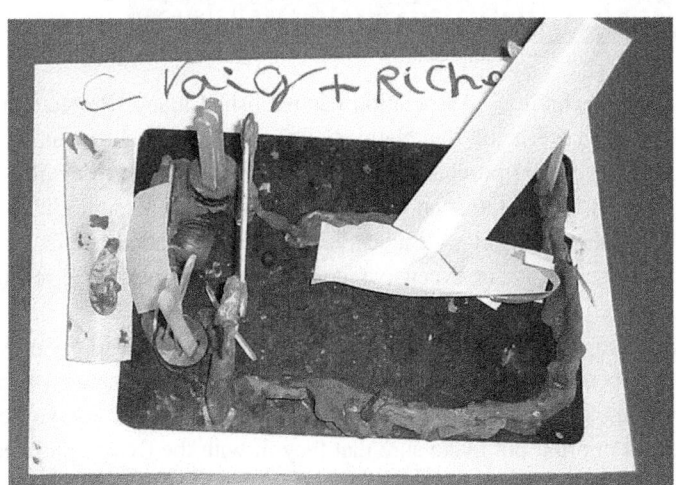

Figure 4.20 Modelling ideas in one medium that will be made in another

ideas produced in quick succession – a three-dimensional version of my 'Multi-design' category.

> **Pause for thought**
>
> Look at Figure 4.21, which shows a model of a vehicle made from a construction kit and its counterpart made in consumable resources. Consider the most logical point in this project to ask children to draw ideas – before or after making the construction kit model? Would taking a photo of the model suffice, rather than drawing? What if they printed the photo the following lesson and used that as the starting point for drawing ideas to be made in the consumable materials?

Figure 4.21 Key Stage 2 children can use construction kits to design vehicles with moving parts

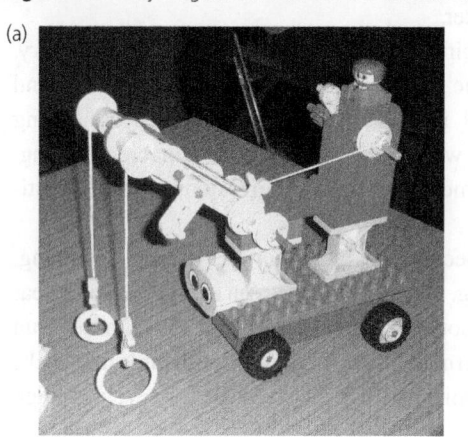

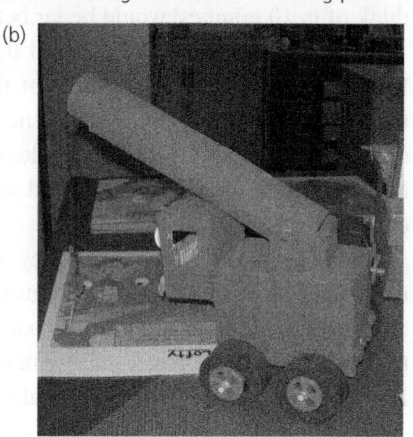

Where to find ideas for projects

The Design and Technology Association has published many 'Projects on a Page' which satisfy the criteria of the National Curriculum for authentic design and technology. These can be purchased from the Association or are available free to members. Check whether the school is a member or if the design and technology subject leader or any of the class teachers have individual membership – or join the Association yourself. It is not expensive, considering how many free resources you can then access.

In the Recommended Reading list for this chapter, I recommend my previous two books plus two books by other authors who convey the holistic nature of learning in design and technology. There are many books of practical ideas that you can mine, both online and in print, but make sure that they fit with the Design and Technology

Association's 'star diagram' (Figure 1.3). Many ideas can be adapted simply by adding the challenge of a user and a purpose. Their suggestions could also be used as Focused Practical Tasks to help children learn techniques and develop skills needed for designing and making their own ideas. These books are often useful for telling you how to make things!

If you are planning your own project, remember that the authenticity of the design process and the final product are important. Give it a reality check.

- How much pretending are the pupils having to do?
- Are the materials authentic?
- How can pupils link the technology to their understanding of science?
- What skills in handling tools, materials and components are being developed?
- Have the pupils looked at real solutions from other times and places?
- How much real designing are they doing? – or is it just limited to the decoration (ugh!).

In order to teach design and technology well, you need to ensure your own competence and capability in handling appropriate materials, tools and equipment – otherwise you may find yourself with health and safety issues on your hands. Always try out the techniques, materials and equipment yourself first, before introducing them to your class. Do not rely on your class teacher or teaching assistant assuring you it will be fine, they did it last year. Make certain for yourself by doing a dry run after school or at home a few days ahead so that you have time to ask questions or make changes to your ideas, if necessary.

Summary

Although this chapter has focused on the practical aspects of making the product, this cannot be separated from the pedagogical underpinnings that were discussed in Chapter 3 or the skills that will be discussed in Chapter 5.

The second half of the chapter looked in turn at each of the main areas of technological activity.

- Structures
- Mechanisms
- Electrical control
- Textiles
- Food

And provided some examples of products that can be made for each one.

Recommended reading

CEE (Children's Engineering Educators) is an American website that has a good range of free resources for design-based technology activities: http://www.childrensengineering.com/freeresources.htm

The following books all have chapters on specific practical areas of design and technology. Although the two books of which I am author were written before the introduction of the present national curriculum, the advice regarding teaching the practical aspects remains the same. All these books should be available in libraries of universities with a Faculty of Education. They can be purchased online.

Flinn, E. (2016) *The Really Useful Primary Design and Technology*. London: Routledge.
Hope, G. (2004) *Teaching Design & Technology, 3–11*. London: Continuum Publishers.
Hope, G. (2006) *Teaching Design and Technology in Key Stages 1 and 2*. Exeter: Learning Matters.
Newton, D. (2005) *Teaching Design and Technology, 3–11*. London: Scholastic Publishers.

Chapter 5
Skills to Develop in Design and Technology

Chapter objectives

- To understand the skills that underlie design and technology activities;
- To appreciate why process skills are important and identify these in relation to design and technology;
- To reflect on one author's classification of design and technology skills and recombine these to develop your own viewpoint.

Introduction

Throughout all the practical activity discussed in Chapter 4, pupils should be using their creativity and imagination to solve problems, considering the needs of others, applying knowledge from other subjects, and developing criticality with regard to existing technologies and towards their own ideas. This is intellectually challenging. This is what design and technology is really all about. It involves rather more than what would be involved in a bit of craft activity on a Friday afternoon – and maybe it is this level of intellectual rigour and challenge that is at the heart of why the subject is not well taught; primary teachers themselves lack these skills in relation to technology and the built environment. This chapter discusses these underlying process skills.

> ### Pause for thought
>
> Many students try to make links between Gardner's (1983) multiple intelligences and design and technology, in the belief that there must be a fit. What would a 'design intelligence' or 'technology intelligence' look like? Try to list some of the features before reading this chapter (you may like to return to this activity after reading the chapter and update your list).
>
> Keirl (2001) maintained this is not as simple as it seems (see link to article in the Recommended Reading list at the end of this chapter). Summarize his main points and consider whether his viewpoint is justified. Note too his critique of the relationship between science and technology. Do you agree with this? Does your opinion affect your response to the rest of his argument?

Why are process (procedural) skills important?

In their report in 2008 to which we referred in the previous chapter, Ofsted said that pupils 'are expected to develop *procedural* capability – "knowing how" – as well as to acquire and apply *propositional* knowledge – "knowing that".' (italics mine). The division of knowledge into declarative (factual) and procedural (process) originates from Herbert Ryle's (1949) classification of knowledge into 'know that' and 'know how' (facts and skills). However, I believe that there is a missing link between the two that is especially important for technological problem-solving: *knowledge of relevance* (Hope 2009).

However good pupils might be at mathematics or however much scientific knowledge they may have acquired, unless they see the *relevance* of this knowledge to the technological problem before them, they will not think to apply it. Therefore, teachers will need to actively encourage their pupils to think about how mathematics can be used or science applied to the technological design problem at hand. The application of knowledge acquired in one subject to a problem in another requires a leap of imagination and the ability to see an analogy between the present situation and something seen in another. Both metaphor and analogy can be rich sources of ideas for finding solutions to design problems, often through 'seeing' the problem differently in the mind's eye.

Problem-solving involves re-applying what is already known to a new situation. There is a strong relationship between problem-solving and what is called 'deep learning', the kind of learning that 'sticks' and promotes real understanding. The practical application of knowledge from a range of fields within a design and technology project reinforces the knowledge from those fields as well as promoting understanding of how this knowledge fits together and how it can be applied in the real world. When solving a problem, something new is learnt about things that are already known: a new application, a new way of doing something or a whole new understanding of how things work or how things might be assembled differently.

Bruner (1985) defined two ways of thought: narrative and paradigmatic, which he saw as two irreducible modes of cognitive functioning. By 'paradigmatic' he meant the kind of factual knowledge epitomized by science and mathematics, which seek empirical truth to verify theory. His 'narrative' mode of thought included not only story, poetry and other forms of literature but also how we make sense of the social world. We seem to want to impose a storyline to all our experiences, real or imagined; we even expect our fantasies to make sense!

But as with Ryle's distinctions, I would argue that Bruner's two modes of thought are not incompatible, as he asserted, because both are needed for designing technology. Narrative and paradigmatic modes of thought become, not just entwined, but essential to each other. Designing technology requires that the product has to work; the mathematics and the science have to be right. However, in having a user and a purpose in mind for every product, there is an implicit narrative, a storyline, behind it all. This kind of problem-solving engages children's emotions, stimulates their empathy with the character (real or imagined) and motivates them to seek a solution. The designed world, based on invention and real-life problem-solving, requires the juggling of many forms of knowledge (including scientific, social, emotional, logical) spanning and interlinking across Bruner's divide.

However, we cannot go too far into the way of saying that the process is everything, and again this comes back to relevance. Younger children (up to about seven years old) find it difficult to identify what is relevant to finding a solution because they do not understand why they cannot change the problem. They have little concept of 'this problem and this problem only' (Donaldson: 1992, p. 135). Donaldson conducted an experiment in which children were shown a dolls' house and a family of dolls who went into the house. She asked the children who was in the house and they were able to tell her. She reached in and removed one of the dolls. Who is in the house now? They could still tell her. One at a time, she removed all of the dolls and the children could still recall who was left. So far, so good; but then, after she removed the last doll and asked the question, many of the children younger than seven years old invented a new character, most often a dog. Donaldson put her hand in the house and pretended to remove the 'dog', whereupon children invented a cat, a budgie, a mouse, a witch – sometimes up to half a dozen new characters. Donaldson concluded:

> They did not have a clear conception of this problem - this one and no other - which they could hold on to and use in deciding when the problem had been successfully dealt with, so that thinking about it should cease. Such a conception is the very foundation of relevance. And there can be no intellectual power where a sense of relevance is lacking. (p. 135)

Pause for thought

How does this impact on the kind of design solutions we should expect pupils in Key Stage 1 to come up with?

An early assessment task for the end of Key Stage 1 in design and technology was to design a rain-hat for a toy teddy bear. The children had to choose appropriate materials and make this hat. Many children preferred to make the hat from the bright yellow shiny paper rather than the piece of black plastic (cut up dustbin bag). I could understand why. Given the choice, I'd rather go out in a nice bright hat and hope it would not rain than be seen in something made out of a black sack. The children had chosen style over practicality. The aim of the game, however, was to pretend that the hat was really going to perform a useful function and so needed to be made from the waterproof material, even if it did look like the kind of thing you'd only put over your head if caught out in a tropical deluge. There was nothing wrong with the children's design skills, they just did not realize there was a sub-plot: only hats made of the waterproof material counted as correct answers to the problem. What was relevant to their minds was the colour and attractiveness of the paper: *what would teddy like to wear?* What was relevant to the test designers was: *can they apply their scientific knowledge to a design task?* Of course, the children knew that a hat made from a black sack would be more waterproof than yellow shiny paper – but if teddy hated his hat he would not wear it anyway, would he? Far better to get drenched than suffer the indignity of having a bit of black sack over your head. And since teddy is not actually, really, going out in the rain anyway, we're just pretending, what's wrong with pretending that shiny yellow paper is waterproof?

> **Pause for thought**
>
> If the hat had been for themselves, what do you think they would have chosen? Does this highlight a basic problem with the task?

I see this as a kind of game-play whose rules young children do not follow because they do not understand that problems have specific rules by which solutions are judged appropriate (or not). Part-way through Year 2, most children have succumbed to accepting that however illogical the game-rules set up by the teacher, these are the ones that must be obeyed. No self-respecting Year 3 pupil would make a similar error – or would they? *Compare this to Case Study 6.1 in Chapter 6 which is accompanied by extended discussion.*

What is involved in designing and making something that someone else needs or wants?

Remind yourself of the Design and Technology Association's memorable definition of design and technology activity (Fig. 1.2 in Chapter 1). Something for someone for some purpose. To design an appropriate product that someone else will be able to use and be pleased with requires *empathy*: the ability to appreciate the perspective of another person. This is something that young children find difficult. Not that they lack a sufficiently sophisticated theory of mind (even toddlers know how to wind up their older siblings), but they cannot place themselves in someone else's shoes and see things from another viewpoint. They assume that everyone else sees things the same way they do.

To develop pupils' ability to see things from the perspective of a potential user of their product, teachers in Key Stage 2 need to present quite specific challenges and a well-defined user, otherwise children can continue to design products that are very generic in appeal or rely too heavily on the pupils' own likes and dislikes.

Ascertaining the needs and wants of the intended user might involve:

- observation and/or discussion, either with the person himself or herself and/or with others involved in trying to solve the same problem;
- research to find out what solutions have already been found to a similar design problem or opportunity and evaluating these to ascertain how well they might apply to this specific person and his or her concerns, circumstances, likes, tastes, style and so on;
- some trial and error in coming up with a viable and acceptable solution, maybe resulting in a drawing, a model or a prototype;
- taking on board feedback from the potential user, from others also working on the same design brief (most probably other pupils) or from experts (most likely the class teacher);
- making a product that their client can actually use and decide if it satisfies the needs/wants of the user.

Designing a product for a user involves:

- *identifying the user's need or want;*
- *evaluating existing designs and products;*
- *generating and developing ideas;*
- *communicating ideas and accepting feedback;*
- *making the product;*
- *evaluating the product and the whole process.*

Note: These six skills do *not* give you a lesson-by-lesson outline for a scheme of work, nor do they even need to follow on from each other in this order. This has been a common mistake in the past, which has dragged out the first four skills so that there is no time left for making a successful product, which will probably take more time than all the other skills put together. Plus: remember that key word, *Iterative,* in the National Curriculum.

Having ideas, talking about them with friends, taking on board their feedback, coming up with more ideas or developing the first good idea, jotting this down or doing a quick drawing, discussing it again, starting to make a model, realizing it does not quite work, doing another quick sketch to work out the details, asking the teacher, looking on the internet for examples, trying to make one of those, talking to someone else who happens to be looking up something similar on the next laptop along the bench, going back and trying again and so on and so on – all this could happen in one lesson. As a teacher, I would want the pupils to have really clarified their ideas and have some record of their decisions about what they want to make by the end of the lesson, so they can go away feeling satisfied but still with ideas buzzing.

If some pupils came back next lesson with something completely different in mind and they could explain to me why they want to abandon their original idea, then I would let them try out the new one and make a prototype of it. I would, however, expect that the majority of the class would be proceeding straight into making their original idea, perhaps with a few tweaks along the way. As a general rule, the younger the children, the closer together the lessons need to be. Year 6 might be able to pick up the threads of their ideas after a week, but Year 3 will struggle and Year 1s will stand no chance whatsoever; they'll just design something new!

Making, modelling, mending, manipulating and modifying

Through an analysis of the children's actions and conversations while using construction kits, my colleague Eric Parkinson identified what he called the '5 Ms' of technological capability, an all-purpose, simple classification of the skills underlying design and technology: Making, Modelling, Mending, Manipulating and Modifying (Parkinson and Hope 2011).

The discussion which follows here in this chapter is my extension and application of Parkinson's insights across a wide range of design and technology contexts. Can you think of skills that do not fit his categories? It is quite easy to produce other words, but they always seem to fall into one or other of the categories that he has already thought of!

Making

The development of practical making skills was, of course, the subject of Chapter 4, so here we present just an overall summary in order to introduce the rest of Parkinson's thesis.

Making is, of course, the part of the technological process that is most obvious to the observer, which is why a whole chapter of this book was dedicated to it. On first sight, therefore, it might be argued that rather than '5 Ms', Parkinson has identified '4 into 1 M', since all the others contribute to the making. This is a valid point but the physical action of cutting, shaping and joining that creates the artefact in real time and space is not usually how the whole process begins. Having an inner image of the intended product or having some possibilities in mind precedes the first action on or with the materials. Even birds can be seen purposefully choosing particular sizes and textures of nest materials. I once watched a swan trawling the bottom of a pond for sticks, which it placed in a pile on the bank and then tested them for flexibility before taking them to its mate sitting on the nest. Evaluation of the suitability of materials for the intended purpose is integral to the construction process. There is much more going on than simply just 'making'; there is purpose, imagination, evaluation, deliberate choice, intuition and more, along with physical skills and knowledge of how materials perform.

There are times when we make something worthwhile by accident but these occasions are usually serendipitous outcomes of some thoughtful experimentation. Even a simple act such as opening the fridge to see what can be put together for lunch has a clear purpose in mind. Successful making requires some prior knowledge of the way in which the chosen materials will perform, both during the making and as a final product. A degree of skill is required in the handling of these materials as well as of the tools used to cut, shape and join them. Moreover, we need to consider the cognitive skills required to visualize the possibilities and constraints inherent in the situation for which our product is intended, to evaluate our own progress towards our goal and the ability to adapt and change ideas, techniques or materials in response to this ongoing evaluation. Finally, there is an aesthetic sense in the making which provides the stimulus to produce a good-looking product, which contributes to the feel-good factor of being pleased with what we have made.

The process of making, therefore, is far more complex than the interaction between hands and tools and materials. However, the development of physical skills, of hand–eye coordination and fine motor skills, is key to a successful and satisfying outcome.

Modelling

Modelling includes all the ways in which people represent their ideas, including thought, speech, text, drawing, computerized simulation, as well as making a representation of something in the everyday sense of the word 'model'. Roberts, Archer and Baynes (1991) called modelling the 'language of design' which can be used for purposes of generating and developing ideas, experimenting and evaluating possibilities, and also communicating those ideas to others. See Recommended Reading at the end of this chapter.

Roberts et al. identified two forms of modelling in relation to design and technology:

Modelling of = *making a representation of something that already exists;*
Modelling for = *making a representation of something that is intended to exist in the future.*

Some examples of *modelling of* within technological activity are:

- Drawing something to clarify what is required before beginning to come up with innovative solutions, for example, what do people need to keep them dry when waiting at the bus stop? Note: below age seven years, most children's 'design drawings' will be of this clarification type;
- Making a range of different types of mechanisms (e.g. levers) in order to develop the knowledge needed to decide which is most suitable for the intended design idea;

- Making a schematic diagram or representation of something that already exists in order to understand how it works, for example, using a construction kit to make a fairground ride in preparation for designing one to be made in consumable resources;
- (A personal recent example) Drawing onto squared paper a complex cable knitting pattern in a form that I could follow as I knitted my jumper.

These kinds of modelling activities have an important place in design development. It is difficult to imagine a new and creative solution without some basic knowledge of how a system works. *Modelling of* can be a useful tool in gaining this understanding.

However, in order to design something new, *modelling for* is the skill that is needed. This requires the ability to use one system to mimic the intended system in some salient way; for instance, the ability to develop three-dimensional ideas through a two-dimensional drawing and to be able to see through the drawing as if it were three-dimensional. The skill of using drawing for modelling ideas is a key skill for professional designers. Using computer packages to do this assumes the same skill in relating two- and three-dimensional forms and being able to manipulate the one to design the other.

The ability to analyse and evaluate forms or ideas represented in one medium to be made in another, whether modelling *of* or *for*, is an essential but often assumed skill. Questions such as 'Would this idea work?' can come through looking at a *model of* something (a drawing, perhaps, or a prototype made in card) or through *modelling for* as ideas flow and are evaluated, modified and developed.

Language is an essential modelling tool and one which is frequently overlooked when discussing designing. However, most design ideas are expressed through talk, especially in the most tentative *modelling for*. These can be identified by sentences that begin….

'I've got this sort of idea that … ..'
'Maybe what you could do is… …'
'Why don't we try… .'

This kind of design thinking aloud is a powerful means of clarifying, generating, developing and evaluating ideas. The design and technology classroom should never be a silent place. I was once doing a comparative study involving two parallel classes of Year 3 children. Class 3P did not talk as they drew their initial ideas; class 3L did. When each class began to make their ideas, two very different scenarios developed. The children in 3P began to do their real designing once they got the materials in their hands. They came up with some exciting ideas but many of these did not really satisfy the design brief. Class 3L, who actually carried on drawing for much longer, produced a far greater range of ideas, which to a far greater extent also satisfied the needs of the user and the requirements of the task. They had been using some of those phrases listed above while they were generating and developing ideas through drawing. Not all their ideas matched their drawings; this did not matter. They had used the drawings as part of the design conversation, to support their thinking and spark ideas off each other, while also keeping each other to the design brief: 'No, because what it needs to do is …' The generation of ideas requires some kind of framework in which these ideas can be developed, tested and refined. This may be through talking, drawing, a construction kit, a computer package or the hands-on interaction with materials.

Manipulating

Parkinson uses the word 'manipulating' to refer to the 'physical acts of children as they combine and shape materials with their hands or tools' but it can also be used to refer to the manipulating of ideas and possibilities in the mind's eye and in conjunction with physical systems. In that sense, 'manipulating' can be seen as closely linked to modelling in its more sophisticated form.

In the physical sense, manipulating relates to the development of hand–eye coordination and to fine motor skills. Anyone who has watched a small baby lying on its back gazing up at a range of small toys hanging from a frame will have observed it reaching towards these objects. Even at six months of age, getting one's hand to the right place seems to require concentration. A major developmental stage is being able to pass an object from one hand to the other. Toddlers learn to take objects out of things (such as emptying the shopping all over the floor) and later, to put objects into containers (but not necessarily the right ones).

Through basic manipulations of objects, important ideas about the physical world are established. The continued popularity of toys with parts that move, turn, make sounds and so on is not just because they are fun. All this play is informing the young child's mind about how they can manipulate the world of physical objects for their own pleasure and purposes (Figure 5.1); Jack is repeatedly retrieving a ball from the end of a run and putting it back into the top. Frankie's bus and its people is much simpler but offers story-making potential.

By the time children start school, they have developed a wide repertoire of fine motor skills that will enable them to manipulate a range of simple tools for making products of their own imagining. They are able to manipulate ideas, decide which would be best and suggest improvements. They can also, of course, manipulate people and this developing social sense is vital for designing a product that will satisfy the wants and needs of a user. Again, around age six to seven years seems to be the developmental point here.

Technological design involves the combination of all of these three kinds of manipulation:

- *of thoughts and ideas,*
- *of physical objects and materials,*
- *of social knowledge.*

Figure 5.1 Toddlers Jack (a) and Frankie (b) explore fitting small objects inside larger ones

Pause for thought

In Case Study 5.1, Kyle (aged 10) is juggling all three. As you read this case study, identify what is the problem for Kyle. What is he trying to achieve and what is defeating him? If you were his teacher, how would you help him to move his ideas forward?

CASE STUDY 5.1

Kyle is sitting staring into space. His class has been asked to design a new bridge to take traffic across the river not far from his school. Everyone knows about the long queues of buses, cars and lorries that back up from the old bridge in the centre of town. His teacher has given the class lots of photos of bridges to give them ideas. Everyone else is talking, drawing, having ideas, one group is already trying out ideas with a construction kit. Kyle has a blank piece of paper.

His teacher, Mrs. McT, has been watching him for a while and decides it's time to see if he's just daydreaming or actually thinking some ideas through: 'How's it going, Kyle?'.

Kyle: Well, I was thinking, either we'd need to have lots of bridges, at least three, or it will have to be one huge great bridge with different levels and things.

Mrs. McT: Explain.

Kyle: Near Cambridge, where my cousins live, there's this Busway thing, like a railway only for buses. Nothing else can go on it, except bikes along the path next to it. A bridge just for buses would be good; they wouldn't be late then. And people could cycle and walk across it too, on the side, like, next to the buses.

Mrs. McT: Ok, but what about the cars and lorries?

Kyle: That's the problem. Perhaps they'd need to go upstairs, like in this picture.

Mrs. McT: Well, they're on a higher level, not actually upstairs.

Kyle: Would that work? Having buses underneath and cars on top?

Mrs. McT: Why don't you try it out? Do you want to draw it first?

Kyle: No, I want to do it over there with Matt. *(nodding towards the group with the construction kits)*

Some time later. Kyle throws down his work with the construction kit.

Mrs. McT: What's wrong, Kyle?

Kyle: It won't work.

Mrs. McT: What won't work?

Kyle: The struts are all the wrong length. Anyway, the bridge wouldn't work. It's too high. How would the cars get up there? You'd need to dig up half the High Street to get a slope that cars could drive up. And you can't do that 'cos of all the shops and the station and everything.

Matt (Kyle's friend): Or have a spiral like in a multi-storage [sic] car park.

Kyle: But you can't make that out of this, can you? It's all straight bits.

Pause for thought

Kyle is manipulating ideas based on personal knowledge as well as photographs. He attempts to model his ideas using a construction kit but after manipulating the pieces for some time, he rejects the result, based on his realization of the lack of practicality of the design and his social knowledge about what people would want their town centre to be like. He cannot take up his friend Matt's idea because the kit Kyle is using cannot be manipulated into the shape Matt suggests. What would you suggest to him to do next?

Mending

Although we would usually use the word 'mending' for actions such as that shown in Figure 5.2 (ITE students experiencing the joys and frustrations of using construction kits) or in the sense of repairing something that has worn out due to long or wrong

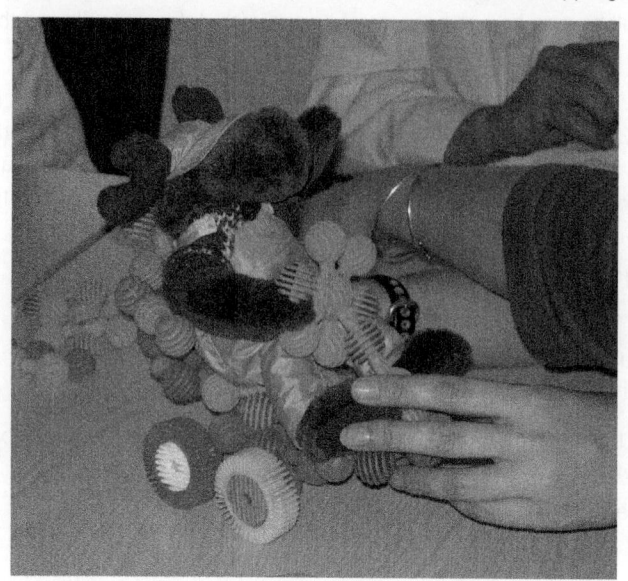

Figure 5.2 A bit of hasty mending and the toy will sit in his car without it toppling over

use, Parkinson also applies the word to any kind of 'fixing' that takes place as the ideas and construction processes fail to live up to expectations.

Like each of Parkinson's '5 Ms', mending occurs within technological development processes carried out by adults and children alike. Mending can be in the physical sense, as parts come loose, the glue dries without sticking two edges together, the wrong materials are chosen, and so on; the innumerable mistakes in construction caused by lack of experience or expertise. Models may fail to meet the anticipated performance criteria as Kyle discovered in Case Study 5.1 and ideas may need to be reviewed and repaired. Perhaps seeing the higher level of the two-level road bridge as 'upstairs' had given Kyle a false metaphor on which to work. Stairs can be quite compact in the amount of horizontal space they take up, and it was not until he built his bridge with the construction kit that Kyle was able to realize on how slight a gradient (and, hence, how long) a run-up to a bridge would need to be, requiring the demolition of half the High Street and the Town Hall which stood on the far side of the square at the foot of the bridge.

From about seven to eight years of age, children begin to place increasing demands on themselves to create products that mirror reality to a greater and greater extent. Gone are the days when they were happy to pretend that the wheels of the bus go round; now they must go round properly and be able to convey the bus down a slope, preferably faster than everyone else's.

In using construction kits, mending goes almost unnoticed since these actions are rapid, complete and carry no trace of repair. This is far less so with consumable resources and this is one reason for encouraging children to draw their ideas before they begin to cut up materials that might be in limited supply. Mending ideas on paper is much less expensive and leads to much less disappointment in the long run.

Although children may be disappointed when their ideas or products do not work, failure, repair and modification are all part of the iterative cycle of learning through technological construction. Seeing why something has not worked may lead to deeper learning and understanding about a mechanism than if the system worked the first time through serendipity. The second and subsequent uses of the same mechanism are unlikely to fail for the same reason. Deep learning enables variations and different applications of similar processes in future, simply because that level of thinking and reflection has caused fuller understanding to take place.

Modifying

When ideas are not working, when plans fail and ideas do not live up to hopes and expectations, there are two options – discard or modify. Modifying applies the mantra 'reuse, reclaim, recycle' to design projects, and adds the creative potential of coming up with totally new ideas. Some of what has been thought, developed or made can straightforwardly be reused, especially if the project or idea only needs a little modifying – perhaps a neater finish, a different choice of glue. Or, perhaps, while generating ideas, a basically good design just needs something extra or different to make it really exciting. Previously discarded ideas or partly made first attempts could be reclaimed ('Where did I put that bit I had earlier – oh, no, I screwed it up and threw it in the bin …'). This is where keeping notes, drawings, diagrams or photos of work in progress is always such a good idea. Previous threads of thought can be revisited and reclaimed. Recycling can be of ideas as well as of physical objects or materials.

Those three principles of 're-use, reclaim, recycle' underlie all skills development. When we learn a new skill, our hands learn the movements necessary to carry it out but each time we repeat the skill, the neural pathways are reused and reinforced. However, we often find ourselves needing to reclaim ones that have not been used for a while and then recycle them in different forms in new circumstances and applications. Learning to crochet, for instance, is really difficult for the first few stitches but slowly the eye, hand and brain get into the routine of what to do and persistence produces a long line of chain stitch. Once it is realized that all other stitches are based on this simple chain loop, this act is modified and recycled endlessly. Even if this skill has not been performed for years, the hand–eye–mind coordination can be reclaimed and reused.

Having the imagination and creativity to modify ideas and products is at the heart of design capability. If everything that did not work properly had been discarded, little technological progress would have been made. There must have been millennia way back in prehistory when, if a knapped flint got blunt it was just discarded for another sharp flake, but at some time or other a creative individual realized that a quick blow to the blade held in the hand would restore the tool to sharpness. Evaluation leading to modification leads to a higher form of thinking and acting on the world. We humans have the capability to see potential applications in things that have outlived or even failed in their original function. For instance, a plastic coating designed for use in the first spacecraft is still in use for non-stick pans decades after its first purpose was abandoned. The glue on sticky notes was a reject – the paper could be peeled off again easily; what a shame? No – what potential! Modifying can even mean looking for a whole new application of a good idea, even if, like sticky note glue, it was totally unfit for its originally intended purpose.

Adapting and modifying is what our species does best. This is how we came to take over the globe in the first place. Other species need to evolve their bodies; we evolved our technology. Richard Dawkins coined the word 'meme' (Dawkins 1989) to signify evolving cultural ideas that survive, mutate and get transmitted between minds through speech, writing and other symbols, and in physical artefacts. This can be as simple as clothing ourselves with another animal's fur in order to keep warm or as complex as seeing how particle physics applies to silica atoms to kick-start the microchip revolution.

Teachers assume that children can see the potential in found objects, such as cartons, card rolls, yoghurt cartons and so on, to provide the basic forms for a product. For instance, using a cardboard carton as the chassis of a vehicle is a common project for young children. Cutting up the legs of old jeans to make bags is a more radical modification of the found object. It could be argued by extension that the use of materials such as paper, card or plastic sheeting to create a product is also a form of modification – a change of the material from a flat sheet into a three-dimensional object through cutting, folding, bending and joining. On this view, modifying is one of the most basic skills of design and technology as a range of different materials, components and ingredients are changed into products through modification and combination.

Observing children at play, we can see this natural urge to modify the form, use and application of toys, construction kits and found objects or materials. Parkinson observed that the construction kit provided feedback as to what can be *played*; that children were almost having a conversation with the kit as they were playing and making. Kyle, in Case Study 5.1, was frustrated that the kit he was using could not support his ideas. However, he was not expecting to use the kit as younger children do, enacting make-believe scenarios as they make, mend and modify the models as their play-narrative develops through the interaction between the kit parts and their imagination.

My own children consumed an endless supply of cardboard boxes in their make-believe play so that I had to always bring the groceries home in a box and remember whose turn it was! I assumed this was universal until I decided to ask my Year 3 class to use their experience and write about what could be made from a large cardboard box. One girl came up to me and said 'I don't think I've ever played with a cardboard box.' I thought this was very sad; what potential fun and creative play opportunities she had missed! *Do you agree?*

Pause for thought

Look at Figure 5.3 showing a torch made by a primary school pupil and 2 puppets made as demonstration resources for my ITE students by a design and technology technician.

List all the components that have been reused, reclaimed and recycled to make each product. The torch actually works, so consider what might be inside, which cannot be seen in the photograph.

How much modification of the reused resources was needed to make each fit for purpose in its new role in these products?

Figure 5.3 Using recycled and/or reclaimed resources

(a)

(b)

There are, I believe, two forms of technological creativity:

- What can I use for this? > On the spot search for something suitable;
- What can I use this for? > Hoarding!

People who regularly make things usually have a supply of hoarded resources to which they can apply the first question. I confess to having more knitting wool, fabric, buttons, trimmings and so on than I can possibly use before arthritis and/or senility take hold. However, when my daughter-in-law wants a mending job done, I can nearly always find the resources to do it.

> **Pause for thought**
>
> Draw a concept map like the one in Figure 5.4, then look back over the whole chapter and map onto the diagram the process skills that have been identified (look into the discussions of Parkinson's '5 Ms'; do not just map his headings!).

Figure 5.4 Concept map for reflective activity

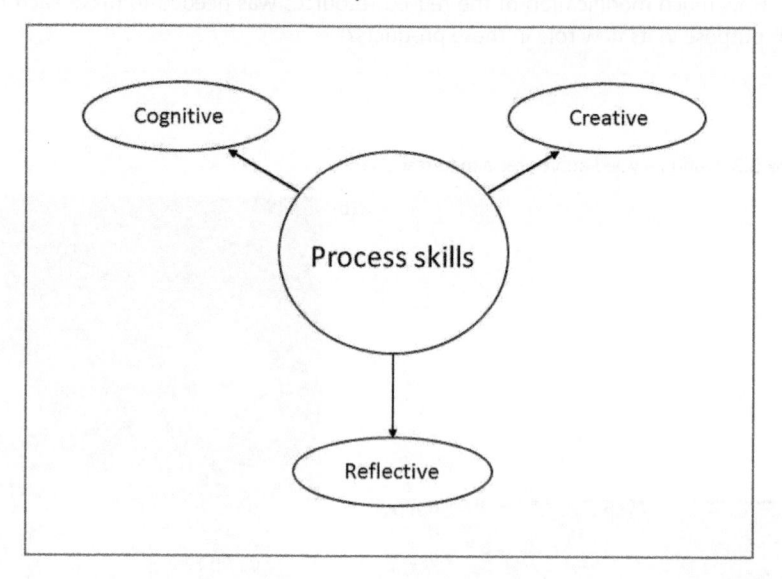

```
        Cognitive              Creative
              \               /
               \             /
              Process skills
                    |
                    |
                Reflective
```

You may find you want to place some skills in two places and draw double-pointed arrows to link these areas. If you decide that some skills are sub-skills of others, just add an extra node. You may also think of process skills that have not been discussed or are only mentioned in passing but that you feel are very important. That's fine – just add another (or more) arms to the 'process skills' area in the centre.

If you are able, compare yours to that of a friend or colleague. How are the two diagrams different and why? Explain to each other your underlying thinking in placing each skill where you have and how you have linked them.

Figure 5.5 shows examples by two students on different ITE courses.

- How do each of them compare to yours? As you examine them in detail, can you see their thought processes and the reasoning behind where they have placed the process skills? How different are they to each other?
- Have they omitted skills? Have you? Have either of them added anything that is not specifically discussed in the chapter? Have you?
- Compare where each of them have placed 'making'. Did Vicky decide that it was another skill, whereas George decided it was central to everything? Where did you place 'making' and why?

Figure 5.5 Two examples of student responses to the task of expanding Figure 5.4: (a) Vicky's concept map; (b) George's concept map

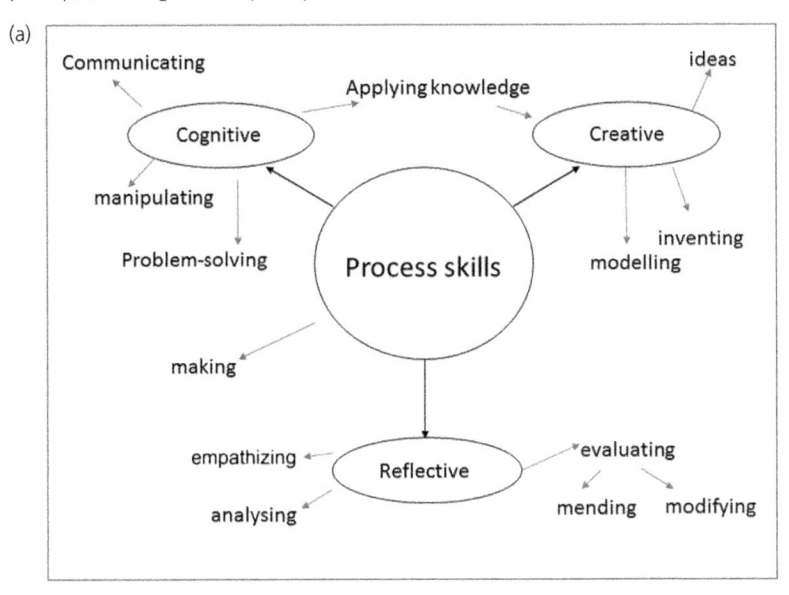

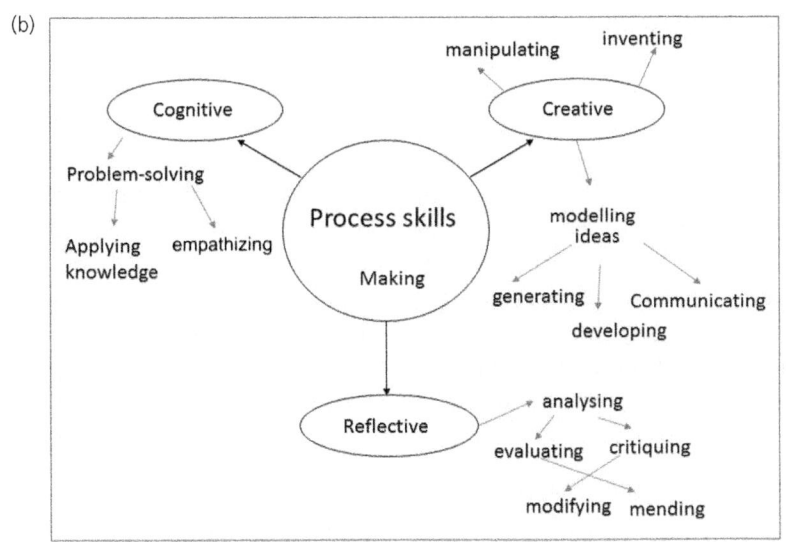

(a) Vicky's concept map shows Process skills at the center, connected to three outer nodes: Cognitive (with related terms: Communicating, Applying knowledge, manipulating, Problem-solving, making), Creative (with related terms: ideas, inventing, modelling), and Reflective (with related terms: empathizing, analysing, evaluating, mending, modifying).

(b) George's concept map shows Process skills at the center, connected to: Cognitive (with related terms: Problem-solving, Applying knowledge, empathizing), Creative (with related terms: manipulating, inventing, modelling, ideas, generating, developing, Communicating), Making, and Reflective (with related terms: analysing, evaluating, critiquing, modifying, mending).

- Vicky has placed 'empathizing' as a reflective skill, whereas George classifies it as a cognitive skill. Who do you agree with (if you agree with either of them) and why?
- Vicky has put 'applying knowledge' as a sort of 'bridge' between cognitive and creative skills (note the direction of her arrows). What do you think of this? Is she thinking about the role of analogy here, perhaps?

- George has tried to suggest the interaction between different reflective skills, whereas Vicky has separated them out. Whose analysis do you prefer?
- Vicky has put 'communicating' as an off-shoot from cognitive ('because language is there, in your mind'); George, on the other hand, has put it as a modelling skill ('that's what my dt teacher used to tell us'). Whose choice is closest to your own opinion? Could both be right? (even though I'm not very impressed with George's answer; he should have a reason of his own, not just repeat what he's been told without critiquing it).

There are no right or wrong answers here, of course, and your friends' concept maps and yours are just as good and just as flawed as Vicky's and George's. This is the perennial problem with complex issues: we can never get to one right answer (often we cannot even get to one *agreed* answer). This is just like designing – there are no absolutes. Answers to design problems can be better or worse, an improvement or not, waiting for someone else to come along and make more modifications to suit new users with different needs, wants and purposes in mind.

Summary

This chapter has considered the underlying process skills in design and technology, using Parkinson's '5 Ms' – Making, Modelling, Mending, Manipulating and Modifying – which constitute the basic hand–eye–brain processes that underlie all design and technology activities. The title of the paper in which these '5Ms' were published includes the term 'technological literacy', a term not much used in the UK but widely used in other parts of the world. It is an interesting term because it includes technological capability in the sense not only of design-and-make but also of understanding the role of technology in society and everyday life. This will become a major theme in the next chapter.

We concluded this chapter by thinking about things a little differently with an activity to cause you to think about:

- the *cognitive skills* that are involved in these processes;
- the *creative skills* required for innovation and invention;
- the *reflective skills* that enable evaluation at each stage of the process.

These are overlapping and intertwining foundation skills and separating them out is not necessarily straightforward.

Recommended reading

Keirl, S. (2002). Hedgehogs, Foxes, Crows and other 'intelligent' beings: Explorations of the Relationship Between Multiple Intelligence Theory and Design and Technology; available at http://research.gold.ac.uk/9655/1/0380208TERCmi%26D%26T.pdf

Parkinson, E. and Hope, G. (2011). *Children, Construction and Technological Literacy* in Stables, K., Benson, C. and de Vries, M., (2011) *Perspectives on Learning in Design and Technology Education, Proceedings of the PATT25:CRIPT8 Conference, London, July 1-5 2011*, Technology Education Research Unit, Goldsmiths, University of London.

Roberts, P., Archer, B. and Baynes, K. (1991). Modelling the Language of Design; available at https://dspace.lboro.ac.uk/dspace-jspui/bitstream/2134/1689/3/roberts_archer_baynes.pdf

Chapter 6
Children's Ideas – Promoting Curiosity

Chapter objectives

The aim of this chapter is to help you to:

- Appreciate the playful creativity of young children;
- Consider ways to stimulate children's curiosity about the made world;
- Use existing artefacts to inform pupils' designing and making of their own products.

Introduction

Young children have all sorts of wonderful ideas about how the world works; I was once assured by a five-year-old that thunder is God moving his furniture about upstairs. Children are naturally curious but also naturally imaginative. They fill up the gaps in their knowledge with flights of imagination (as we all do, really – but it is rather more noticeable with young children).

Since design and technology is about designing and making real products for real users that really function, we immediately find a clash between the freewheeling world of the young child's imagination and the hard-nosed need for realism at all cost. However, in order to invent an innovative product one requires the ability to think outside the box, the ability to play with ideas and see new applications of existing systems and artefacts, and the creativity to juggle reality with fantasy.

Pause for thought

The link to Frederik et al.'s (2011) article can be found in the Recommended Reading list at the end of this chapter.

The authors begin with a statement about 'technological literacy', a term which is sometimes used to refer to capability with technology and also understanding its impact on our lives. How do the authors say that understanding technological artefacts contributes to both these aspects?

Children's curiosity and imagination

Children are naturally curious creatures and this curiosity surfaces early. Figure 6.1 shows Lily moments after she was born (with no awareness of the technological world into which she has come) and Ella aged five months, still unable to lift her body off the floor, but already exploring one of her sister Frankie's toys.

For the first two years of life, 'playing' is mainly a matter of exploring things, for instance:

- emptying cupboards,
- putting things inside one another,
- throwing things,
- climbing in, up, over, through ….

and so on.

Around age two a change begins to happen, first of all role-playing familiar routines (e.g. putting a doll to bed), and then the imagination just seems to take off (e.g. pretending different-sized objects are 'mummy' and 'baby' and making them talk to each other, which Frankie would do with everything from cutlery to bottles of cleaning products). By age four, they want to join their ideas with those of others and inhabit a socially constructed imaginary world. They have also ceased to get so frustrated when things do not fit, balance, work just how they want them to; they have started to accept the limitations of the real world. However, within the world of their imagination, anything can happen. For instance, on seeing a well as a garden feature in one of my neighbour's gardens, four-year-old Frankie stood transfixed, making a long wish – that she could fly.

The artist Paul Klee longed to be able to recapture this innocent childhood world with its freshness of vision but it is impossible. The young child is genuinely seeing everything new and can imagine any number of possibilities that adults know cannot be the case. Across the primary school years, we see children develop from the wide-eyed to the realist.

Figure 6.1 From unawareness to active investigation in less than five months

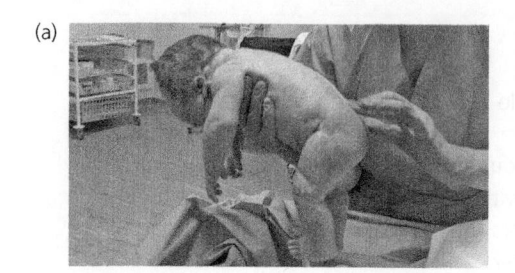

Teacher: How could we help the seeds in the dark cupboard grow?
Child: I'll paint a picture of the sun and give it to them.
Such stuff as dreams are made of!

Playfulness and design capability

The ability to create an inner fantasy world is readily observed in the play of small children. Their fantasy worlds are absolutely vital for developing design skills and children with rich internal play-scapes make good designers. In developing a play-scape, however fantastical it might be, the child creates and applies an internal logic that coheres the whole construct of his or her imagination. Strange creatures may inhabit this fantasy world but they act within the constraints of the whole. Characters play out their roles logically and usually consistently; the backdrop may remain constant over many weeks or months.

This creative construct within the child's imaginative life demands the same skills as designing: to reason within a logically coherent system, to generate problems and questions and attempt to bring them to a satisfying conclusion. As a mental process, thinking through a design solution is no different to playing out how to rescue two plastic figurines from a couple of fire-breathing dragons on a sinking island. Learning to play the design game requires understanding that the product needs to satisfy the design brief and also be creative within the parameters of the design criteria. Key Stage 1 children struggle to understand that they must work within the rules that the teacher's definition of the 'game' implies – and are then confused when the teacher rejects their interpretation, adaptation or development of the game. Case Study 6.1 illustrates this.

> ### CASE STUDY 6.1
>
> Ms. de S asked her Year 1 class to design a travel bag for Fred, the class teddy. The children are streetwise enough to recognize that Ms. de S is only pretending teddy is going on holiday somewhere and needs a bag for his imaginary possessions. Ms. de S has provided only paper, card and cloth to make the bag and glue to hold it all together (but the children know that bags are not just glued together, they have seams on the inside, so more pretending will have to be done here). However, it turns out that Ms. de S is not prepared to accept Zhen simply pretending the bag will open, it really has to. Plus, she is not very interested in all of Annie's paper cut-outs of things teddy might need such as sunglasses and sunscreen, although she seems delighted with Sam who cut a couple of tickets out of bits of card that Sefraz dropped on the floor on the way to the bin.

> **Pause for thought**
>
> What is the fantasy situation that Ms. De S has set up? What is the reality of the design solution she expects?

The children's perspective, however, is: We're playing Let's Pretend teddy is going on holiday and needs a bag. It does not need to open as we can pretend that bit. We can also make some play-props from paper (sunglasses etc.) as part of this making-for-play. We know how to do all this because it's the kind of game we play all the time. Our teacher Ms. de S is pretending some things and not others, so we are not sure what we are allowed to pretend and what we are not.

As children get older, they learn to perceive the game that the teacher is playing and to fit their creative problem-solving into that framework. Lower Key Stage 2 pupils would have little difficulty playing along with Ms. de S's teddy's travel bag design task. They would make something that fit properly over the teddy's arm and could be opened to store his tickets, rain mac and other holiday essentials. It is sometimes said that children lose their early creativity as they get older and schools are sometimes blamed for this. Personally, I believe this is a natural maturation process as children have to learn to come to terms with reality and channel their creativity into solving real problems. The free-flowing world of Let's Pretend has to be squared with the real world of everyday life.

Let's Pretend play comes to a finale as a child spends more time setting up and making play-props than he or she does playing the game for which the props were intended. Elaborate backdrops may be assembled, a host of props made from recycled resources, signs, invitations, letters may be written and the whole assemblage is imaginative, logical and fit for purpose. The conclusion comes when the child is satiated, yet no game is played with it. There is little difference in engagement between this making-for-play and the process of designing a product for someone else to use. A clear goal is in sight, the activity is purposeful and focused, progress is evaluated and adaptations made to bring results into line with the needs of the imagined users. In school, children need to bring their design activity to a conclusion within a specified timeframe, which might limit the flow of ideas but might also focus their mind on achieving the goal. There is satisfaction in the process and, hopefully, also in the product.

As part of a project on homes, working with a Year 1 class, I collected a large number of identical-sized strong card boxes from a local grocery store. These were to be stacked in rows to make an apartment block and the children would work in pairs to fit them out with furniture. Each pair had a jointed plastic toy who was going to 'live' there. Their concept of scaling was interesting. They made chairs that the toy could sit on. The tables looked good except that the chair did not fit underneath when the toy was sitting on it (my suggestion that 'Maybe it's a coffee table' seemed to get around this problem).

However, for me, the most interesting discovery they made was that when the toy was sitting on its chair, it could not fit inside the box! My suggestion that we all turn the boxes the other way around so the furniture and toys all fitted inside was greeted with groans and protest – some groups had already coloured the inside of their box with 'carpet' and drawn pictures on the walls. They were much happier just pretending that the toys could sit on the chairs inside the room.

Was this an invalid project? I do not believe that. The children discovered something about the problem of having two parameters: big enough for the toy to use yet small enough to fit in the 'apartment'. Making the table high enough was a sufficient challenge for many, especially since some of the pairs had made a decision about division of labour: 'You make the table and I'll make the chair.'

Technically, what they made were models but for the children, these were real products. My 'apartment block' idea did not get far. They were constantly wanting to take their own one out of the stack to play with it on the floor alongside their friends' ones. The toys would visit each other and move the furniture outside so they could sit out. Some toys soon owned cut-out paper plates and cups to lay on their tables.

A play-prop/toy is a real product in the eyes of a child, as are:

- a swing for a Princess who exists only in the imagination;
- a vehicle for Prince Charming to get to the ball (Cinders has the coach, so how did he get there?);
- a spaceship for a mouse to fetch cheese from the moon after the rest of the mice had eaten every last morsel in the whole wide world.

just as much as are tarts for the Queen who does not like hearts or any other storyline teachers invent to link the design and technology lesson in with the Book of the Week.

> **Pause for thought**
>
> This issue is discussed by McLain et al.'s (2016) article 'Traditional tales and imaginary contexts in primary design and technology: a case study' (the weblink is listed in the Recommended Reading list at the end of this chapter).

Most Year 1 pupils are very aware of the difference between 'real' and 'pretend' and they are more than happy to play 'Let's pretend' when asked to design products, although they may not respect the teacher's definition of what is to be pretended and what must really function. They have little problem understanding the world of make-believe, and are less concerned about the hard-facts reality that we value so much as adults. They are happy to pretend that what they have to hand is whatever their imagination decides it will be. However, this is not a clear-cut division. Young children can get very upset if the play-prop they are designing and making does not function with sufficient reality to play its role. A door cut into a cardboard box has to open and shut properly; it may even require a split pin to make a door handle.

As children get older, of course, the greater the level of reality they will expect to achieve and that teachers should expect of them. By age nine, many pupils will expect their products to really work, although they will still be willing to engage in playful flights of imagination in terms of the user and purpose for which their product is intended. By the end of Key Stage 2, most projects should lead to a real product for a real user, although I would still consider planning an Olympic stadium as a valid outcome of a design and technology project for Upper Key Stage 2. After all, architects present models to their clients in the hope they will get the commission for the real build.

Fun, fantasy and imagination are the essential ingredients of childhood and creatives everywhere. If we are going to foster imagination through design and technology, we need to not only be creative in the projects we plan and the design briefs we present to our pupils but also in our acceptance of their response to them.

> **Pause for thought**
>
> Watch the video clip of Key Stage 2 pupils designing a swimming bag for members of a local swimming club, available at http://www.bbc.co.uk/education/clips/zxq8hv4. This project is most certainly focused on the real world of real people needing a real bag rather than the fantasy of teddy going on holiday. But – will the children really produce something the ladies will actually use?

How closely should the final outcome satisfy the design brief?

Simple answer: closely.

If a teacher has asked their pupils to design something for a particular user and purpose, then designing something for someone else or for a different purpose (or none) will not really answer the problem they were asked to solve, however 'creative' or aesthetic the outcome might be. The word 'creative' is in quote marks here – often the word is used just to mean 'different from expectations'. There is a world of difference between finding a creative working solution to a design problem and simply making something that is not like everybody else's.

Zara (Year 2) was the catalyst for my personal epiphany about creativity in design and technology. She was always 'off-task' producing something unusual. Was she very creative or did she not understand the need to solve the problem as set? It affected other curriculum areas too. After we went around the school field looking for signs of spring, she drew a diagram of potatoes growing underground: 'Did we see any potatoes?'; 'No, but I know how they grow.' Case Study 6.2 is an example of her work in design and technology.

CASE STUDY 6.2 Zara's Easter Egg packaging

Each child was supplied with a section of wide card tubing. The design brief was to make this into an Easter Egg holder that would be attractive to a customer but also hold the egg securely. A range of plastic cups, small pots, cotton wool, bubble wrap, were available, plus they were able to help themselves to anything else in the 'Mr. Junk' box.

Zara's solution was to turn the tube on its side, make a hole in the side for the egg to fit into and then attach string to each end so that the whole product could be worn over the shoulder like a bag. Her teacher (me) was bemused and challenged. It was different, divergent – but was this *creative*? She had not grappled with the problem in the way that I expected. Was I just being a spoilsport?

Zara's product did not answer the design brief. The egg was not held securely; the product did not even stand upright, it rolled over with the weight of the egg. If it were worn like a bag, chocolate could end up smeared all up the wearer's clothes. It was 'interesting', definitely different, but a creative solution to the design brief – no (sorry) – it was not fit for purpose.

Pause for thought

Why did I decide that although Zara's response was imaginative, it was not an innovative solution to the problem as set? Am I being harsh or does this underlie the difference between art and design and technology?

Using children's curiosity about the technological world

This section of this chapter looks at the way in which examining existing products can stimulate children's imaginations and give them ideas for what they would like to make. This is not a case of providing a pattern and saying to pupils 'We are all going to make one of these.' Rather, the products that are shown to pupils should be seen as starting points for developing their own ideas and making their own product. Children can look carefully at existing products to get ideas for what they want to make. Often children will begin to generate design ideas as they do this and this should be encouraged. Older children should have a notebook handy to jot these ideas down, either in words or pictures.

Strong cross-curricular links can be made through looking at existing technologies, their development and impact. The national curriculums for both history and science list examples of inventors who should be studied. The history curriculum begins with the Neolithic, the time at which humans transformed their way of life through new ways of thinking and the creative application of technology. We humans have transformed the planet through our technology; there are very few wild places with no human footprint; we even left some on the moon. This means that links can be made to the geography curriculum as pupils learn about technological solutions to landscape problems (e.g. bridges), transportation problems (roads, ships, railways) or social problems (housing, food and water resources, sources of heat and power).

Children's natural curiosity about the world around them frequently leads them to ask questions that are difficult to answer in a way that they could understand. Children need to understand the role of technology in the development of human society and our dependence on it in our daily lives – and learn to critique this realistically. There are moral and ethical issues here, not just practical ones. The plastic bottles we discard can be harmful to local wildlife and oil spills devastate huge areas of coastline. Yet, medical technology can provide a means by which a paralysed man can move his hands again and communications technology can notify the rest of the world about famine and enable the mobilization of relief. Pupils need to understand that the development and application of technology is a choice made by people who want something better than what they have already (however 'better' might be defined) but that sometimes this may lead to choices that might not be made by people in other circumstances or may cause problems for other species or environmental systems.

> ### Pause for thought
> The South African National Curriculum for Technology has a section entitled 'Technology and Society' which deals with these kinds of issues, which the National Curriculum for England does not. Look at the excerpt from this part of the South Africa National Curriculum for Technology (below). Have you seen these kinds of issues included in design briefs that are set to pupils?

The learner will be able to demonstrate an understanding of the interrelationships between science, technology, society and the environment.

There are three specific areas:

- indigenous technology and culture;
- the impact of technology; and
- bias in technology.

The learner can be given opportunities to explore these issues within the contexts of particular needs. For example:

- Indigenous technology can be explored within the context of the need for people to drink safe water.
- The impact of technology can be explored within the same context; the learner can be made aware, for instance, of the difficulties people will experience in

dry areas and how their lives can be changed if technology is used to supply safe water.
- Bias can be explored by looking at the difficulties some groups of people might have in collecting water from remote supplies, or how taps may be difficult for the disabled, old or very young to turn on.

These 'needs-based' opportunities are ideal for integrating with the 'investigating', particularly when the learner is finding out about background contexts, the people concerned, the environmental situation, and so on.

These same issues should also be dealt with directly when designing. The learner should be given specifications and constraints to guide design ideas. These should include aspects relating to people, impact and bias. These same criteria should also carry on to the evaluation stage, where the learner should use them to evaluate his or her own products. (Department of Education, Pretoria (2002) pp. 18–19)

This raises some interesting questions about the design briefs that teachers give to children especially in relation to users. To what extent do teachers ask children to identify these social issues and design a product for someone who is handicapped by age or by a physical disability or mental difficulty? A whole new aspect is then introduced to the design problem: it is not just for anyone, it is for an elderly lady who needs to use crutches to get about indoors or for a small child who is unaware of dangers and so on. Thinking of a specific user (or specific group of users) also enables a much more tightly focused investigation of existing artefacts. The next section of this chapter discusses the types and sources of suitable collections of these that could be used in the classroom to stimulate ideas and discussion.

Product collections

Real designers do not start with a blank sheet of paper or with no knowledge of what already exists. All designers start with an in-depth study of existing solutions to similar problems and consider how these might apply to the one they are now facing. Children's design capability is severely limited if they are asked to make something without looking at existing products and solutions. They need to have studied and evaluated ones that already exist in order to understand how they are made and to what extent these might be incorporated or adapted into their own work.

For each project that is planned, it is useful to have a selection of products and/or samples that can be used to support pupils' designing and making. These do not need to be vast collections or contain large products that are difficult to store. For some projects, just one product will suffice. Nor do they need to contain examples of what the pupils will actually make. For instance, a teacher may be able to rely on pupils' knowledge of hand or finger puppets and simply introduce to the class the puppet theatre and the storyline for which they will make them.

Not every collection needs to be a box of real products. You might:

- Supply non-fiction books, photographs or videos;
- Ask your pupils to search the internet;
- Use the local environment;
- Invite a craftsperson or tradesperson to bring the tools of their trade, the products that they make, and talk about how design decisions are made and how/if these are recorded.

Although there is nothing quite like seeing and handling real products, photos can successfully be used and may even be more appropriate:

- When pupils will be making small-scale models of much larger structures that cannot be brought into the classroom;
- For showing a range of products from around the world;
- For showing historical artefacts;
- For showing work by another class – perhaps from a previous year but also from another school if you have a friend whose class has already done a similar project.

Creating a product collection does not necessarily involve a great deal of expense. Charity shops are excellent sources of bags, toys, ceramics, picture frames as well as interesting clothing such as sequinned evening wear, shawls and scarves – but be careful, your informal spending can soon add up. Check whether these kinds of purchases can be reimbursed and keep your receipts. All second-hand products need to be washed but then so should all donations of clothing and fabrics to schools.

Three creative teachers:

- Joel persuaded his Mum to dress up in an outlandishly glamourous number and do a few twirls and ask his Year 3 class to design a bag to go with the outfit.
- Maxine asked her friend Ravina to demonstrate to her Year 1 class how a sari was put on and worn.
- Sabrina's aunt had her own business making glamourous evening dresses and she was happy to save the off-cuts for Sabrina's Year 5 class to decorate cushion covers.

Pause for thought

Do you have friends and/or relations who could supply expertise, artefacts, or both, who would be willing to come into your classroom? Do you know a retired teacher who would be willing to come into your class?

A product collection could include examples made by yourself or your friends. For instance, if, as part of your university course, one of the practical sessions involved making the kind of toys shown in Figures 4.10 and 4.11 (in Chapter 4), and you immediately see the potential for making these in your upcoming school placement, arrange to borrow several from your friends and take as many photos of everyone else's as you can, including work in progress. Your pupils will love the show and enjoy handling the products. It will give real impact to your teaching and real impetus to their designing.

You do not need to source all these collections yourself; use other people's collections! Local museums should be the first stop in finding out about industry and commerce in your town. Sunderland Museum, for instance, has real 'Wow factor', with rooms about coal-mining, ship-building, textiles, pottery and more. Since the building is shared by the public library, they have thoughtfully placed a rack of books about each subject in each room. Many local museums have many more artefacts in store than on display and will advise you on what else your pupils can see and handle on a pre-booked visit. Some will loan collections to schools or an education officer may be able to visit. Heritage centres often offer similar experiences and make a real effort to connect with local schools. It is worth enquiring. Places such as Chatham Historic Dockyard, Kent, or the Black Country Living Museum in the West Midlands provide such a rich learning experience that it is better to visit them.

Using pupils' knowledge and experience

You should always try to use your pupils' existing product knowledge. For instance, you can rely on all pupils knowing about toys. Those designed for young children often contain mechanisms that can be applied in other contexts. Figure 6.2 shows an example of a toy used to stimulate discussion and ideas for making 'toys with noise'. The upright sections in the tummy bump on the floor and each other as it goes along and this makes a clackety sound.

A toy such as Ella's pull-along (Figure 6.2) can be used to stimulate questions about how else a toy could make a sound as it moves along and evoke a range of responses and ideas which pupils could discuss with one another, drawing on their own knowledge of similar toys. More ideas will come if time is given to experiment with suitable resources such as metal bottle tops, lolly sticks, beads and pebbles to put into metal and plastic containers or to be strung on strings, and so on, to spark imagination and new ideas. Taking photos at this stage is an efficient way of recording ideas to be shared on-screen at the start of the next lesson to stimulate designing a 'toy with noise' for a toddler.

Figure 6.2 Ella's pull-along toy

> **Pause for thought**
>
> Jack's pull-along spider (Figure 6.3) bounces up and down as it is pulled along – how do you think it does it? If you have access to a similar toy, examine it carefully. Are the axles central to the wheels or eccentric (not central)? Do the wheels rotate freely on the axles or are they fixed? Do the axles rotate or move in any way?

The axle/wheel configuration of the spider is complex but examining it can stimulate pupil discussion about:

- How are wheels attached on other toys?
- Do they just spin on their axles or are some firmly attached (for instance on battery-powered toys)?
- What about the 'pull back and let go' kind of toy car?
- Are front wheels sometimes attached differently to back wheels?

Most boys in the class will be experts here; use their knowledge, ladies, it is probably going to be far more up-to-date and detailed than yours! They will also be more than willing to bring in examples but be warned: you may need to allow them half-an-hour's play time with them before being able to focus their minds on using them as a design resource and you may have to be lenient towards those who cannot resist a quick play from time to time. Making a joke of it helps but showing real interest in

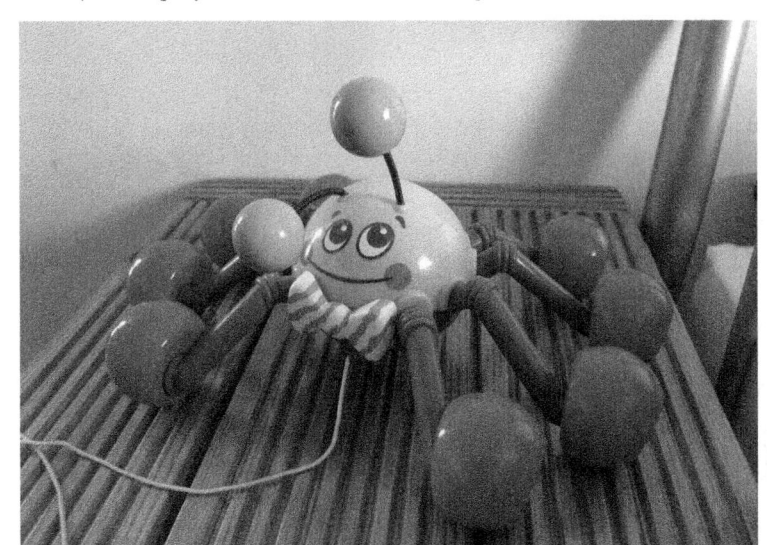

Figure 6.3 A pull-along toy that bounces as it moves along

their toys is better. They'll appreciate it and be more willing to play your game in return and design a drag racer for an alien or whatever.

Using the local environment

Teachers are adept at seeing the potential of the local environment as a resource for history, geography, religious education and even, occasionally, science, but sometimes miss the opportunities for using it as a resource for design and technology, yet schools are surrounded by the built environment; railway lines, supermarkets, bridges and even canals may be just round the corner or down the road.

Pause for thought

View the following video of a class visit to the Clifton Suspension Bridge near Bristol, designed by Isambard Kingdom Brunel:

http://www.proteachersvideo.com/Programme/3196/ks2-design-and-technology-a-taste-for-bridges

Watch again the first few minutes (up to the point where one of the boys reacts strongly to realizing the bridge moves) and identify:

- The learning gained from the visit that could not be gained by learning about the bridge in the classroom, either before or after the visit;

- The level of emotional engagement shown by the children over and above a classroom-only experience;
- What the teacher watching the video gained from observing the visit;
- Think about a similar structure or notable building in a locality near you – how might you use it as a basis for design and technology learning? Be specific about the age range of the pupils. Would it be suitable for Key Stage 1, Lower or Upper Key Stage 2?
- What cross-curricular learning is also taking place in the visit to the Clifton Suspension Bridge? What cross-curricular learning could be incorporated into a visit to a technological structure in your locality? Again, think specifically: which age group, linking to which parts of the programmes of study for which other subjects?
- What health and safety issues would there be in conducting such a visit?

You may not be able to visit anywhere as spectacular as the Clifton Suspension Bridge but there are ways around this! Case Study 6.3 describes the use that two newly qualified teachers made of both of their local environments.

CASE STUDY 6.3

Anna and Karina had both got jobs working in a Year 5 class in their first year of teaching, so they promised to keep in touch after university. This proved to be very profitable, especially since both were faced with planning a project on frame structures in their first term. Karina was in a small village school in Somerset and Anna was in Hull. Anna was full of confidence about bridges and using her holiday photos of the Golden Gate Bridge and planning to take her class over the Humber Bridge. Karina felt a bit lost. There were only concrete slabs over streams in the middle of muddy fields near where she was working and she'd never been anywhere as impressive as San Francisco. She decided to ask Anna for some help but felt she needed to offer something in return. Why don't we make this a joint project? The children would benefit from each other's experiences and think of all the cross-curricular benefits, especially geography.

They began by using Skype to make contact with the other class. After the first hysterical giggling and cries of 'They talk funny!' both classes settled down to ask each other questions about where they lived.

Anna's trip to the Humber Bridge was planned for the next Tuesday so they agreed to take video footage as well as photos and send these to Karina's class. In return, Karina's class would do an internet search for bridges in all different places. 'Let's see how many different sorts of bridges we can find' said Karina. 'Then we'll try to work out why some of them are frame structures and some are not. Remember, our project is designing frame structures, so we need to work out why people choose to build a bridge that way.'

Anna's class was very much aware of their responsibility in recording as much about the Humber Bridge as possible for the sake of Karina's class. They took photographs, video footage and drew pictures. Some of Karina's class began by saying 'We don't know anything about bridges' but Karina countered this by asking 'Who's ever been over a bridge?' By the next week, her class had assembled an impressive portfolio of pictures of bridges and were especially fascinated by how older bridges, such as the Forth Railway Bridge, were a mass of girders whereas more modern ones, such as the Edinburgh road bridge, were clean sweeps of concrete. 'Let's set that as a challenge to the class in Hull' suggested Karina, mainly because she was foxed by the question herself.

> **Pause for thought**
>
> What is the answer? How does it relate to improved knowledge of structures? What science is involved here?

Figure 6.4 A view across a bridge and the entrance to The Lowry, both at Salford, Greater Manchester

(a) (b)

Like bridges, most large modern buildings are steel frame structures. Often, they are clad with stone or in-filled with concrete blocks but many impressive buildings use the structure as an aesthetic feature and attach glass panels to give the whole area a sense of light and space. Unlike traditional brick or block building, steel framing allows interesting curved shapes to be created (see Figure 6.4).

You could plan for your class to design a 'city of the future'. They could work in small groups to design and make models of specific parts of it, each mounted on strong card, and all put together at the end.

Practical note: Use the small white (cheap) pipe cleaners for creating small-scale frame structures. They can be easily bent but retain their strength, enabling curving structures to be created. Paper straws sold for art work are a second-best choice as they do not readily hold a curve. Rigid materials such as lolly sticks, dowel and paper sticks can only create straight section frames.

While engaged in this project, pupils might learn about brown field sites, the need to check for archaeology, how existing buildings are demolished and recycled, the provision of services, public transport and the way complex technological systems interact. A major new development in your locality may provide the ideal opportunity for a visit. If there is one in progress or even at proposal stage, you may be able to invite an architect, a member of the council planning department or a spokesperson from the construction company to come and talk to your class. Perhaps there were/are objections and someone from a community action group would be willing to come and explain the case against the scheme – but not at the same time as the pro-scheme person; you cannot risk a row in front of the children!

> **Pause for thought**
>
> What potential does the school environment itself have for product analysis? How old are the buildings? What are they made of? If it is a new building, perhaps the architect could be contacted.

How our food is reared, grown, caught, processed and reaches the supermarket

Children's interest in food makes any topic about food production of intrinsic interest. As well as cookery activities, understanding about the food industry enables children to understand the technological geography of their country. The food section of the National Curriculum for England for design and technology clearly states the need for pupils to acquire knowledge of where our food comes from.

Farming is a major industry in the UK so it is essential for children to learn about how their food is cultivated or raised. The Countryside Classroom website has resources for all subjects and Key Stages relating to food production and land management. Resources for design and technology can be found at http://www.countrysideclassroom.org.uk/resources?subjects=design-and-technology

In all parts of the country there are farms that welcome school parties and some major urban areas have city farms, such as Mudchute Park and Farm on the isle of Dogs in East London, whose website states,

> The Mudchute education project provides a unique resource for schools and local children. The project works with local schools by providing structured activities and courses in environmental education, science and farming topics. These are linked to the needs of the National Curriculum ...
>
> https://www.mudchute.org/childrens-young-people-services/mudchute-education

A follow-up activity of a visit to a farm with a large number of sheep could be to make felt from a fleece. A list of all sources of fleeces can be found at http://www.woolsack.org/BWFleeces. Instructions for felt-making can easily be found online too.

Visiting arable farms is less well publicized but many farms have diversified into providing facilities for visitors. Farms shops, farms that grow Christmas trees or pumpkins, or farms that grow mainly fruit may be willing to host a visit. Village schools have an advantage here, of course, and teachers in urban schools might consider forming a partnership with a village school to the mutual benefit of both (as in Case Study 6.3). A local agricultural college may have a schools' outreach programme or study centres such as the National Fruit Collection at Brogdale, Kent which has an educational programme (http://www.brogdalecollections.org).

Fishing is also a major industry, both wild-catch and farmed. Schools in coastal areas with a fishing fleet can make cross-curricular links with both history and geography in a local study. The fish-farming industry sometimes gets bad press, suggesting that it is responsible for polluting the seas around our coast. This is not necessarily the case and research in the Shetland Islands has demonstrated a far greater diversity of invertebrates below the salmon cages than in areas that are trawled for wild-catch. Shetland (where both salmon and mussels have been farmed for many decades) and the North Atlantic Fisheries College, whose researchers monitor the environmental impact of both ocean fishing and fish-farming, is at the forefront of marine spatial planning worldwide.

Using knowledge from other curriculum areas

Creative designing does not mean that the children have to produce all the ideas out of their own heads; real designers do not do that. They search online or look at existing products and solutions for inspiration. They will use knowledge of mathematics or science, parallels in other cultures, look at historical precedents, use computer graphics or artistic genres. This means, basically, that designers (children or adults) can use whatever is appropriate for any given design situation.

Cross-curriculum connections are always a good thing since they underline the holistic nature of human knowledge; the real world is not divided neatly into history, geography, technology and so on. However, simply pulling in learning opportunities from other curriculum areas and asking children to make something does not guarantee high-quality design and technology experience or learning. What may be missing is the *designing*. Making a copy of a historical artefact or something used by people in another part of the world is a practical activity in a history or geography lesson, *not* design and technology because the pupils' innovative designing opportunities are minimal.

The Top 3 prizes on my personal horror list go to:

- 'ancient Egyptian cuffs' (what??) For a start, the things that tomb paintings show round Egyptian wrists are bangles, not cuffs. Cuffs are things on the ends of sleeves – and the ancient Egyptians did not wear sleeves. A bit of slightly curved card with randomly drawn hieroglyphics fixed around the wrist with sticky tape has nothing whatsoever to do with design and technology. Nor does 'design a tomb for a pharaoh' – how morbid. Do you really want children waking up in the night with terrors of being stuck inside one?
- Making 'Tudor houses' out of shoeboxes and setting them alight to replicate the Great Fire of London – which occurred in 1666, that is, fifty years after the death of Elizabeth I (the last Tudor monarch).
- Design a canoe for a Plains Indian. There were no rivers on the Plains and, in any case, since these peoples' ancestors were migrants from cities whose surroundings became a desert, it is unlikely that they had ever seen any sort of boat.

And no cardboard models of Viking ships either – very limited design opportunity here; Viking ship design cannot be improved upon (see Fig. 4.2 and commentary in Chapter 4). No design opportunity in making shadoofs either. Yes, they are ancient technology and pupils should learn about them in a history lesson but do not call it 'design and make'. Much more exciting would be to make one large, properly working model of one. Far more exciting and memorable than a whole batch of identical tiny shadoofs littering the windowsill. Your pupils can then lift real buckets of water with it. I once made a full (child)-sized model of a Saxon hut in the middle of my classroom, using the huge card tubes that carpets come on, covered with strips of sugar paper to represent thatch. The children loved it and played Anglo-Saxons in it endlessly. The table-top model of a Saxon village that they subsequently created and played with also taught them a great deal about life in the early Middle Ages.

Pause for thought

Have you seen activities like these in schools? Were there any design opportunities? What were the children learning from these activities? Did it promote their curiosity about these historic artefacts?

However, historical and geographical artefacts are effective starting points for creative design and technology. For instance, many cultures produce stunning textiles (including West Africa and Malaysia). This is a perfect opportunity to combine geography with art to inform a design and technology project. For instance, making a bag inspired by West African textiles to showcase the vibrancy of present-day West African culture.

https://en.wikipedia.org/wiki/African_textiles provides a useful overview of the history and variety of West African textiles. However, the majority of West African textiles available in the West are the 'Dutch Wax' printed fabrics (so called because it is believed that the technique was introduced by the early Dutch traders). Examples of these can be seen at http://africanqueenfabrics.com/

The 2014 National Curriculum for England for history for primary schools begins with the Neolithic revolution which changed people from hunter-gatherers into settled farmers. This technological, social and economic revolution happened independently in at least four different parts of the world. Living in permanent settlements transformed the relationship between people and the landscape – and also with other species. Settlement meant people needed to build more permanent dwellings and acquired more possessions (and needed storage facilities to keep them in). The ground needed digging, hoeing and weeding; crops needed irrigation, tying to stakes, protecting from other species (insects, birds, mammals, fungi, viruses and bacteria). Larger yields led to larger-scale harvesting, storing and processing. It was one of the biggest technological revolutions in the history of mankind. You cannot teach children about the Neolithic without teaching them about the technology – and not just the new tools and artefacts but also of the systems of organization and transportation which rapidly developed once people began to live and farm on the same land for generations.

Summary

This chapter has had a twofold focus:

- Stimulating children's ideas for a range of products;
- Using existing artefacts to enable pupils' understanding of the technological world and to provide ideas for their own work.

In doing so, we have explored the interaction between curiosity and playfulness, fantasy and reality. The National Curriculum for England for Design and Technology encourages an examination of existing products in order to stimulate and inform design ideas. In Chapter 2, we noted that the Design and Technology Association promotes investigating existing artefacts (IEAs) as an essential part of the whole process. However, before doing so, we looked at the South African National Curriculum's section on Technology and Society and suggested that this kind of evaluation of existing products should take place in order to enable pupils to design an effective product for a specific user for a specific purpose. Much poor designing is often caused by lack of such specificity in the design brief.

Recommended reading

Frederik, I., Sonneveld, W. and de Vries, M. J. (2011) Teaching and learning the nature of technical artifacts. *International Journal of Technology Design Education*. Available at https://link.springer.com/article/10.1007/s10798-010-9119-3

Hope (2005). *The Types of Drawings that Young Children Produce in Response to Design Tasks* in *Design and Technology Education: An International Journal*, 10(1); Design and Technology Association, Wellesbourne, Warwickshire. Available at https://ojs.lboro.ac.uk/ojs/index.php/DATE/article/view/Journal_10.1_2005_RES3/112

McLain, M., McLain, M., Tsai, J., Martin, M., Bell, D. and Wooff, D. (2016). *Traditional Tales and Imaginary Contexts in Primary Design and Technology: A Case Study*. Available at https://repository.edgehill.ac.uk/8921/1/Traditional%20tales%20and%20imaginary%20contexts%20in%20primary%20design%20and%20technolog%20%20%20.pdf

Chapter 7
Assessing Children in Design and Technology

Chapter objectives

This chapter will enable readers to:

- Understand assessment for learning in design and technology;
- Appreciate the link between creative teaching and creative learning;
- Identify progression in design and technology;
- Consider how designing technological solutions can develop child autonomy and agency;
- Encourage pupils to realistically evaluate their own work and achievement through self- and peer-assessment.

Design and technology lessons should encourage children to be creative and to seek innovative solutions to practical problems – but how do we plan lessons that enable such creativity and problem-solving and (an even thornier problem) how do we assess them? The aim of this chapter is to answer these questions as well as planning how to ensure progress and set up an effective and rigorous framework for assessing pupil learning. As you read this chapter, you should be able to make links with the principles of good pedagogy underlying planning and assessment across all subjects in the curriculum.

Effective assessment of pupil progress in design and technology needs to be addressed urgently in schools in England. It has been identified by Ofsted (2016) as an area of national weakness:

> In most cases, schools had not yet developed an approach to assessing pupils' achievement in D&T in line with the new national curriculum because of the priority given to English and mathematics. Leaders had not defined the precise skills and knowledge they expected pupils to acquire in the subject at the end of each project or over time. Therefore, teachers were not well placed to judge how well pupils need for pupils to have opportunities to practise and had achieved or what their next steps should be. (Ofsted 2016)

Assessment for learning

The model of assessment that is adopted in this chapter is that of assessment *for* learning. Assessment *of* learning may be informative but unless it has the purpose of enabling teachers to plan effectively for pupils to progress their knowledge, skills and understanding, it is worthless. Ensuring pupil progress through effective planning and assessment is the essence of effective teaching. The planning and assessment cycle (Figure 7.1) should always be held in mind.

When reading this familiar diagram, students often assume that the process starts at the top – with planning. This is not quite true. It is great to have a wonderfully creative idea about what might be taught but the whole thing will fall flat unless it keys into what the children are able to achieve – and the only way to know that is by assessment first. Now this does not mean formal assessment (i.e. some kind of test); it will involve a combination of:

- looking at examples of the pupils' previous work and/or observing them doing a similar activity, especially the one that precedes your lesson;
- consulting the class teacher's (or previous class teachers') assessment records;
- discussing the viability of your ideas with your class teacher, mentor, the design and technology subject leader or university tutor.

Lesson planning needs to take account of pupils' prior learning. When visiting students on school placement, I would sometimes read the plan of the first lesson of a series and find no reference to prior learning. I would ask: How do you know it is

Figure 7.1 Planning and assessment cycle

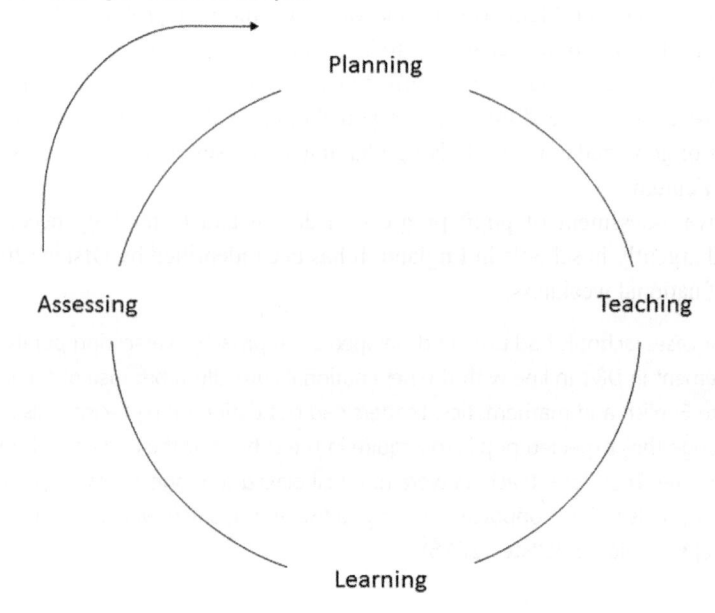

aimed at the right level? The student would look at me bemused: 'But I haven't taught them anything about it yet.' Children are not empty vessels. Pupils come to a first lesson on a topic with a whole range of experiences and memories of those previous experiences, along with skills and capabilities learnt at home as well as at school. The question is: how do teachers know that their pupils will be able to learn what they are planning to teach them? How does it build on what those pupils can do already?

For instance:

- Have they used these materials, tools and equipment before?
- Have they had experience of any of the cutting, shaping and joining techniques?
- Do they know about relevant health and safety issues?
- Do they know your signal to stop and put down tools immediately?
- If they will be drawing or modelling their ideas in another medium before beginning to make their product, how much experience of working this way do they have?
- If they are going to be working in groups, how experienced are they in doing this in design and technology?

These questions are especially important if you are planning to do something innovative (introduce a new way of working, for instance). There needs to be sufficient continuity with what the children are accustomed to doing for them to be able to take on board your new ideas and be successful the first time around. The last thing you want is for your class to end the lesson in a state of disappointed frustration (and for yourself to go home in a state of despondency vowing never to try anything like that ever again). So – think through and record all aspects of your plan that you believe they will be able to handle with confidence because they have the skills/knowledge already, and do not try too much innovation all in one go; spread it over several lessons and build it up in clear steps.

You need to be clear with your pupils what the success criteria are for each of your lessons – and stick to them. You can commend pupils who have excelled on other aspects but you cannot criticize those who have failed to do something if you have omitted to ask them to do it. Which means that safe and sensible working practices need to be on every list. The Design and Technology Association's 'star diagram' (Fig. 1.3 in Chapter 1) is the ideal assessment tool; remember to make it clear to your pupils which of its six essential aspects you are particularly focusing on in this lesson.

Assessing your own learning

An essential part of becoming an effective practitioner is to be realistically honest about how well your lesson has gone and what you might want to consider in future. Consider recording 'Teacher's Learning' as well as 'Children's Learning' in your reflections on the success of a lesson. Using sticky notes is the easiest way to record these reflections. As your lesson progresses, you might quickly jot down things that occur to you that are going well, or that you need to change, reiterate or build on in the next lesson. A good example of this is illustrated in Case Study 7.1. Suze was a confident student on her final school placement in a mixed Year 3–4 class, trying out some whole class teaching of design and technology for the first time. She is going to be in charge of the saws and Mrs. J, her teaching assistant, will be helping generally.

> **Pause for thought**
>
> As you read Case Study 7.1, consider:
>
> - How did Suze promote trust in her leadership in the lesson, while also providing the opportunity for gaining a child's-eye view on her planning and organization? Is this a good strategy?
> - What problem of communication led to some pupils misbehaving?
> - What unforeseen problems could have arisen here? (Fortunately, they didn't)

> **CASE STUDY 7.1**
>
> Just before sending the children off to begin making, Suze said: 'Now, you know I haven't taught design and technology in this room or with you before, so there may be things that I haven't put in quite the right places or might even have forgotten altogether! If you spot something or think something could have been done better, write it on a sticky note and stick it on the whiteboard.'
>
> *At the end of the lesson, she said:*
>
> 'and a Thank you to those who remembered to come and tell me how we might organize next week's lesson better. I have here on my pad "Put more split pins in each pot" Thank you, George, that would save me having to go round with more. Here's an interesting one, though, from Carmen: "Have dowel cut the right length so we didn't have to queue up to do it." Now part of my plan was to have you all learn how to use a saw, which is why you had to cut your own but I agree with Carmen, there was a bit too much waiting about and a couple of people got a bit silly while they were waiting and I was concentrating on helping someone else. They had queued up to ask me something when they could have gone and asked Mrs. J.'

Suze had identified an issue with the actions of her teaching assistant but wisely decided that this would be better done when they were discussing the next lesson. Mrs. J also had time to reflect on the lesson and she had identified her uncertainty as to her role as one reason for the problem that led to misbehaviour. When working in a new way or a way unfamiliar to your support staff, it is sensible to be crystal clear what you want them to do. Give them a copy of the lesson plan in good time so that they can raise any concerns. Be clear what your success criteria are. Suze wanted to check that all the children could use the saws but she had failed to make this clear to Mrs. J, who sent two children to her to ask about something completely different, which could have resulted in a health and safety issue.

> ## Pause for thought
>
> As you read Table 7.1 showing the results of the Grainger, Barnes and Scoffham (2004) investigation into creative teaching:
>
> - Which of these characteristics do you feel describes you now?
> - Which do you aspire to?
> - If you had to whittle the 'teachers' and 'pupils' sections down to three points, which would you choose?

High-quality learning in design and technology ticks all the boxes. Good design and technology will not be taught by someone who is not enthusiastic, committed and confident. A confident teacher will plan to give their pupils space to expand and

Table 7.1 Where Grainger et al. (2004) found that creative teaching is likely to flourish

Teachers:	<ul><li>are enthusiastic, committed and confident;</li><li>seek to make connections;</li><li>use flexible teaching styles;</li><li>have a secure knowledge base;</li><li>have access to appropriate resources;</li><li>are working in a supportive environment;</li><li>are aware of how they are creative.</li></ul>
Pupils:	<ul><li>see the purpose of their work;</li><li>are emotionally engaged;</li><li>feel valued and trusted;</li><li>are encouraged to ask questions;</li><li>seek to make connections;</li><li>are encouraged to speculate and take risks;</li><li>are encouraged to reflect on their work;</li><li>work with their peers.</li></ul>
Learning:	<ul><li>is structured around expectations;</li><li>is placed in a values context.</li></ul>

develop their own ideas, to be proud of themselves and their own achievements. They will be building capable learners who can transfer this confidence to other areas of the curriculum.

Deep learning will only happen through joined-up knowledge and design and technology is an excellent vehicle for developing cross-curricular understanding. However, children will not guess this by themselves. It is up to the teacher to draw out that understanding from pupils through skilled questioning – and sometimes that conversation sparks new ideas in teachers' minds too (see Case Study 7.2 for an example of creative teaching).

CASE STUDY 7.2

One cold December day, Jade was working with a group of Year 1 children melting chocolate over a bowl of hot water to make Christmas decorations. As she introduced the word 'melting' to the children, it occurred to her to ask them where they had heard this word before: 'Ice cream' … 'lollies' … 'ice on the school pond', they said. Jade asked 'What about soup when you take it out of the freezer?' They looked blank. Perhaps their Mums did not make batches of soup and freeze it in blocks for another day … 'I'll bring some tomorrow', she said.

On the way home, she noticed some puddles had already frozen. 'I must be mad' she thought as she put a plastic bag and a fish slice in her bag the next day. Jade now had a whole lesson plan focused on freezing, thawing and changing state. A whole science topic had developed out of a simple food technology activity.

Planning for independent learning

In many nursery and reception classes, the young pupils are encouraged to become independent learners who can fetch what they need, make decisions about what they are going to do and to be proud of their developing capabilities. The further up the school one goes, so it sometimes seems, the more limited the range of materials provided, the tighter the design brief, the more uniform the resultant products and the more critical of their own achievements pupils seem to be.

At Meadows School, Southborough, Kent (a residential special school run by Barnardo's), the design and technology teacher, John, has incorporated *independence* into his assessment criteria (see Table 7.2). The rubric for this explains:

> This is the level of differentiated support a pupil needs to achieve the level of work shown in the [progression] grid … and should be taken into account when considering the pupil's overall ability. This way a pupil with Developing Independence may produce the same level of work as a pupil with Mastered Independence but should not be considered to have the same ability.

Table 7.2 John's scale for assessing the development of independent working in design and technology

Beginning	Developing	Approaching	Secure	Extended	Mastered
With significant assistance or prompting, pupil can … .	With some assistance or prompting, can … .	With limited assistance or prompting, can … .	With only periodic advice or support, can … .	With growing independence, can … .	With independence, can … .

I think this is a useful criterion that could feature in mainstream schools' assessment too. The ability to work independently is more than being pupils able to get on by themselves without constantly asking for help. For example, can a pupil:

- remember to follow routines for practical work, such as putting newspaper on tables?
- get out and tidy away materials and equipment correctly without being prompted?
- choose and use appropriate materials and the correct tool for the job?
- take routine health and safety precautions, such as hand-washing, equipping themselves with safety clothing, ensuring hair is tied back etc. without needing to be told?
- listen to, remember and follow instructions without needing to be reminded?
- be aware of the needs of others and take appropriate action (e.g. moving out of the way, helping to hold, carry or support flimsy or large constructions)?

> **Pause for thought**
>
> In 2008, Eric Parkinson and I presented a paper at the British Educational Research Association's conference entitled 'Design across the curriculum: expanding opportunities for pupil agency and creativity'. It was written at a time when the QCA schemes of work were in use in many schools in England and we were especially concerned about the straight-jacketing that this implied.
> Our paper is available at www.leeds.ac.uk/educol/documents/178008.doc
> Identify the factors that teachers felt were limiters to children's agency and creativity. Have things changed? Would we get similar findings today, ten years later? What leads you to this opinion? If possible, discuss this with other students or primary school teachers.

Pupils assessing their own progress

In order to enable pupils to become reflective learners who can realistically assess their own progress, they need to be provided with opportunities for both peer assessment and self-assessment. Although it is usually easier to see where someone else's work needs improvement than one's own, beginning with peer assessment may not always be the most sensitive approach. Bringing one's creative ideas into fruition involves an investment of oneself into the process in the way that completing a worksheet probably does not have.

Teachers need to model peer assessment in the way they ask questions about children's work. An invitation to 'Tell me about what you have been doing; what is this part here?' is a much gentler way of speaking than simply saying 'What is this bit for?', even if you think the child is really way off-task. Likewise, 'How are you doing? Have you worked out how you will …?' allows the pupil to talk about their progress and verbalize their assessment of what has been done and what is still left to do. Suggesting to pupils that they go and look at what someone else has done, or is doing, enables them to benefit from the progress of others.

At the end of a project, a simple tick sheet or 'happy sheet' can enable younger pupils to record how well they feel they have done. Older or more able pupils could write full sentences in response to the questions. However, this is a 10-minute plenary activity, not the focus of a lesson, so plan accordingly. Avoid questions that lead to yes/no answers. Depending on the focus of the lesson, questions could include:

- How well have they completed the assignment for today's lesson?
- How well have they used tools to make the product?
- How well does the product work in the way that it should?
- How pleased are they with the look/finish of the product?
- If they gave it to the intended user right now, how pleased would they be with it?

These questions could also be used as prompts for group feedback and peer assessment. Working in small groups (max. 4 per group), pupils could assess each other's work according to the design brief. Designating one pupil as chairperson who will report back at the end of the discussion will work in Key Stage 2; younger children are prone to have forgotten everything their friends said and ramble on, making it up as they go.

In order to develop their sense of agency and autonomy, Key Stage 2 pupils should be taught to assess the progress of their work across the course of a project. However, when they are deeply involved in designing or making, they will be unwilling to break off in order to write down what they are doing. One way around this is have an in-built 'Reflect Time' within each lesson; about half an hour into the making time is about right. These break-to-think times are important, otherwise pupils can just drift on and not necessarily be progressing well across the whole of the lesson. Have the key points of the design brief and/or success criteria displayed on the white board throughout the lesson and refer back to them at this mini-plenary point. Ask the children to briefly write down (or draw a diagram) of the point they have reached and what they believe they need to do next. This will focus their minds and also provide you with assessment data. A five-minute stop in the middle of making will not necessarily be popular the first time you introduce it but it will soon become part of the routine.

At the end of the lesson have a further five-minute's 'Reflect time' during which they record what they have achieved in this lesson (Key Stage 1 pupils can do this too). You will then have a record of their sense of fulfilment and of their understanding. Do this before you start clearing up, as it is amazing how all thought can evaporate completely during the time it takes to wash a few glue spreaders and fold up some newspaper.

To develop pupil's ability to self-assess their progress, ask questions such as:

- who learnt to do something new today?
- who was helped by someone else to solve a problem or difficulty?
- who had to re-think part of their design and made it much better?
- who has really thought carefully about who their product will be for?
- who has come up with an idea they have never had before?
- who managed to make their product work just like they hoped it would?

This kind of focused questioning reinforces to your pupils their achievement of the learning objectives for the lesson. They are not just 'making something' in a vaguely half-hearted way but see that your expectations were important and you are pleased with those who have achieved these outcomes. You might also refer back to the mini-plenary and mid-lesson 'Reflect Time' and ask who wrote down something they needed to do next and has now done it. This then reinforces your teaching strategy and demonstrates the importance of this mid-lesson review of progress towards the stated goals.

CASE STUDY 7.3

On her final school placement in a Year 6 class, Barbara devised a means of combining a way to developing pupil autonomy that also doubled as an assessment tool. In one corner of the room, she had a 'Help Desk' on which was placed basic materials and equipment they might run out of (sticky tape, staples and so on) but the great innovation was the way she used sticky notes. If pupils felt they had a really good idea about how to solve a problem (measuring, joining, answering the design brief, or whatever) they wrote this on a sticky note, making sure to put their name on it, and stuck the note on a whiteboard behind the Help Desk. If other pupils were having difficulties, they could go and consult the sticky notes and know who to go and ask for some help or advice. If there were no notes that dealt with their problem, they wrote an 'I need help with …' note and rang a little bell which stood on the table. Usually another pupil would respond and come and offer advice and, if successful, 'signed off' the note and put it on the 'solved' side of the board. If no one came to help within a couple of minutes, the pupil rang the bell twice, and Barbara would acknowledge the call for help and go to the pupil's table as soon as she was able. Not only did this make the working atmosphere positive and supportive but, as she said to me after the lesson: 'I have my assessments done.' What did she mean? By looking at those sticky notes, she knew who was able to solve design and practical problems and communicate them with others. She also knew who was less confident in their work and needed help.

Pause for thought

Could Barbara's idea work with younger children? What system might you devise to encourage pupil autonomy? Could this also feed into pupil assessment?

At the end of a project that has been spread over several lessons, there should be some kind of celebration or display of everyone's work. You need to plan this in, because you do not want to end that final lesson in a rush and have no time for taking photographs or sharing achievement. Having everyone showing their work individually to the whole class can take a long time. Better to have a 'Gallery Walk' in which all work is displayed on tables and everyone walks around to admire everything. Some teachers choose a different group to show their work at the end of each project but this can cause discontent among those who have to wait most of the year for their turn (forgotten they ever had a turn). Groups could give feedback to each other by choosing just one pupil from each group to share their work with the whole class, after which the other members of the group explains why they have chosen this piece of work. You will need to monitor whose work gets chosen each time in case there is some popularity voting going on and it may also be wise to choose some yourself for 'special mention' on a range of hidden criteria, such as really trying hard when it looked like the whole project was doomed at some point in the process.

Pupils should be allowed to take their work home, because parents need to see and appreciate their children's developing practical capabilities, but the work should stay in the classroom for a few days for everyone to enjoy. You might consider inviting another class to come and visit (a 'Private view', like at real galleries!). However, this should either be a parallel class that has been working on a similar project or younger children who will be impressed by the higher standard of work than they themselves are capable of just yet, rather than older pupils who might respond with 'We did that last year', which might dampen the spirits of your current creative geniuses.

Progression in pupil learning

Your pupils will not make progress in their learning unless you as their teacher understand the way in which knowledge, skills and understanding can and should develop in design and technology. The Design and Technology Association and the Expert Subject Advisory Group (ESAG) for design and technology have produced a Progression Framework to explain the expectations across each Key Stage, which is downloadable from the Design and Technology Association's website at https://www.data.org.uk/resource-shop/primary/design-and-technology-progression-framework/

For Key Stage 1, the Progression Framework indicates knowledge and skills to develop across the Key Stage. However, for Key Stage 2 you will see that as well as listing knowledge and skills to develop 'across the key stage' there is a sub-division of skills into 'early' and 'late' Key Stage 2. This recognizes that whereas some

Table 7.3 Excerpt from the design and technology Progression Framework

| Understanding contexts, users and purposes | Across KS1 pupils should:
• work confidently within a range of contexts, such as imaginary, story-based, home, school, gardens, playgrounds, local community, industry and the wider environment
• state what products they are designing and making
• say whether their products are for themselves or other users
• describe what their products are for
• say how their products will work
• say how they will make their products suitable for their intended users
• use simple design criteria to help develop their ideas | Across KS2 pupils should:
• work confidently within a range of contexts, such as the home, school, leisure, culture, enterprise, industry and the wider environment
• describe the purpose of their products
• indicate the design features of their products that will appeal to intended users
• explain how particular parts of their products work

In early KS2 pupils should also:
• gather information about the needs and wants of particular individuals and groups
• develop their own design criteria and use these to inform their ideas

In late KS2 pupils should also:
• carry out research, using surveys, interviews, questionnaires and web-based resources
• identify the needs, wants, preferences and values of particular individuals and groups
• develop a simple design specification to guide their thinking |

elements of children's learning need slow development across the whole four years of Key Stage 2, for other skills clear markers can be laid down part-way through the Key Stage. Table 7.3 is taken from this Framework.

The Design and Technology Association has published Projects on a Page that were written to fit into this Progression Framework and thus to enable the effective delivery of the National Curriculum. If you look at ideas and/or schemes of work on other websites, check that all the skills specified in the Association's Progression Framework will be covered. If not, then adapt the scheme so that they do – or look elsewhere.

After teaching your lesson(s), you will want to know if it was successful in developing pupils' learning. The Design and Technology Association has published a document concerning formative assessment. Note that the Assessment Guidance document is titled 'formative assessment', which accords with the model of assessment for learning with which this chapter began. This is available at https://www.data.org.uk/resource-shop/primary/formative-assessment-initial-guidance/

Consulting both the Progression Framework and this Assessment Guidance before planning your lesson(s) will help to ensure that your expectations of your pupils are realistic.

CASE STUDY 7.4

John devised a Project Template booklet for his Key Stage 2–4 pupils in the special school in which he works. This contains all the pages John might want to use for any project – but (*IMPORTANT!*) he does not use all the pages for every project. This would be overkill in terms of the amount of paperwork for each project and not all of the pages are relevant to any specific project. John constructs a booklet for each project from this template by deleting and/or adapting the pages. Some projects use only a few of the pages. Together with the photo record, the booklet provides supporting evidence of each pupil's work and progress.

Figure 7.2 shows the instructions on one of the sheets of the Template Booklet that he devised to guide his pupils through the project (*layout adapted*).

Some teachers, like John, find a pre-printed booklet helpful, providing a unity of format and understanding to develop across the school. Others provide a design and technology notebook in which pupils draw their design ideas and into which photos of finished products and other supporting paperwork can be pasted. This keeps everything together in one place but someone has to do the pasting. Also, it is difficult to keep a book clean while working with messy materials such as paint and glue, so the book (and the ideas it contains) ends up being kept off the working table; thereby defeating the principle of the iterative development of design ideas.

Individual sheets of paper are far better for working out designs as these are low-stakes if mistakes are made. They can also be easily to hand on the working table and

Figure 7.2 Instructions for flow diagram to enable pupils to track their progress through a project

Flow diagram

Use the start of the flow diagram below to plan/track your making of the metal man. *Ovals* are for Start/Finish or the making process, *rectangles* are for processes and *diamonds* are for quality control checks. All quality control checks must have YES and NO answers. Use arrows to connect the boxes. Use extra sheets if you need to.

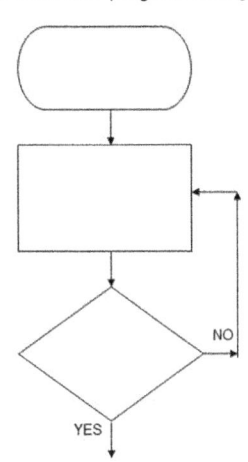

it does not matter if they get glue or paint on them. All sheets, as well as samples, trial pieces and printouts of ideas from the internet and so on, can be stored in a large envelope. At the end of the project, these can be sorted and sifted by the pupil and a 'design story' created and presented in a folder or loose-leaf book. At this stage, work can be annotated (perhaps in a different colour pen or pencil) to provide the opportunity to look back over the whole project and evaluate their thinking and working process. A photo of the final product and a brief comment can be recorded as to its success using the Design and Technology Association's 'star diagram' (Fig. 1.3 in Chapter 1).

Pause for thought

Which would you prefer to use? How helpful would you find it to have a pre-printed booklet like John's? Have you seen something like this in use in a school? Discuss with colleagues the different formats of notebooks, loose sheets kept in folders, and so on, that you have observed. Which format makes assessment the most straightforward?

Longer term planning and assessment

When you first start teaching (or when on school placement) you will only be concerned with planning your own lessons. However, you need to be aware of how your planning fits into the medium- and long-term planning of your Year Group, Key Stage and of the whole school, and how design and technology links with other subjects, especially science and mathematics. A table such as Table 7.4 can help make these links explicit. For instance: are there mathematical skills that need to be taught before the class embarks on an assignment that demands accurate measuring and cutting? Or perhaps you want your pupils to do some trial-and-error investigation ahead of teaching a scientific principle. Do not forget the science of good nutrition as the foundation for food technology. However, it is up to your food technology lessons to ensure that healthy food is fun to make, is well presented on the plate, tastes good and appeals to all the senses. I have not put literacy on this table as speaking, listening, reading, comprehending, recording in labelled diagrams, lists and continuous text, using a word processor and so on will occur constantly across all projects. You should, however, record specific skills that you are embedding in a design and technology lesson to practise and develop these in context, for instance, Year 2 pupils making a list of materials they will need.

As well as making and keeping records of teacher assessment of pupils' progress, evidence needs to be kept. Otherwise, there is no way of knowing how or why a teacher claims a particular pupil or the whole class have achieved a specific skill or level of capability. Ideally, digital storage should be used for record-keeping. It is efficient, space-saving and readily available long after the products have gone home, fallen apart or been eaten! Photos of the progress of a project as well as the final product should be taken, uploaded (and stored by the pupils themselves in KS2, if possible). Each pupil could then choose which photo(s) they want to print and perhaps frame or make into a small booklet to take home.

Table 7.4 Suggested format for recording linking skills across subjects

	Design and technology	Science	Mathematics	Other subjects
Key Stage 1 projects				
Lower Key Stage 2 projects				
Upper Key Stage 2 projects				

Summary

Planning and assessment is a big topic, of which we have only been able to scratch the surface here. Use the Design and Technology Association's materials, since these have been created specifically to support teachers in delivering the National Curriculum for England. However, all schools are different. A project that may succeed well in an urban school may fall flat in a small village or what worked well in a leafy suburb may not be appropriate in an inner-city area. Different schools have different levels of educational needs as well as capabilities. This can vary between Year Groups and classes too. Parallel classes, to which children were allocated randomly on entry to the school, may not be parallel at all. One may have far more children with great imaginations, whereas the other seems to be filled with those who 'don't know what to do, Miss'. All children have the entitlement to a great education – tailored to their needs, wants and capabilities. Your plans will need to be adapted to cater to them – but not your assessment criteria. At the most basic and practical level, their next teacher needs to know where they will be starting from. In terms of portraying the big picture, you cannot fudge it; you do need to say it as it is – but it is also up to you to show progression and demonstrate that your teaching has been a success, which means that evidence-based record-keeping is absolutely essential for your peace of mind and that of your colleagues and management team.

This chapter has stressed:

- the importance of assessment for learning and the role of formative assessment in that process;
- the help available from the Design and Technology Association;
- the link between creative teaching and creative learning;
- the importance of pupils being involved in the assessment of their own progress and its link to independent learning.

An extended example from an expert teacher in Kent has been provided.

Recommended reading

Resources from the Design and Technology Association:

- Progression Framework

  https://www.data.org.uk/resource-shop/primary/design-and-technology-progression-framework/

- Formative assessment

  https://www.data.org.uk/resource-shop/primary/formative-assessment-initial-guidance/

Parkinson, E. F. and Hope, G. (2008). 'Design across the Curriculum: Expanding opportunities for pupil agency and creativity'. Available at www.leeds.ac.uk/educol/documents/178008.doc

Chapter 8
Practical Issues

Chapter objectives

In this chapter you will:

- Learn about support available from the Design and Technology Association;
- Understand health and safety issues that you need to consider when teaching the subject;
- Apply understanding of inclusion and diversity to design and technology;
- Learn how to be proactive in your professional development.

Introduction

The aim of this book has been to inspire you to want to teach really high-quality design and technology and to equip you with the understanding needed to be able to do so. This final chapter deals with the practical issues of classroom delivery of the subject – but always with a look towards your future professional development. This is why it begins with an overview of the minimum requirements for a school to deliver design and technology and ends with the question: What if they ask me to lead the subject?

Throughout this book, you will have found many references to the help, support and guidance of the Design and Technology Association's excellent materials. This is deliberate. The Design and Technology Association really is the one-stop shop for everything related to design and technology. They are the national professional organization for design and technology in the UK with individual and corporate expertise going back decades. They have been instrumental in encouraging research, advising government ministers as well as teachers, developing courses and resources written by experts, promoting excellent practice in schools. They were the prime movers in writing the design and technology curriculum for the 2014 National Curriculum for England, so they really understand what its intentions are.

Figure 8.1 The Design and Technology Association Expert Subject Advisory Group's 'jigsaw diagram'

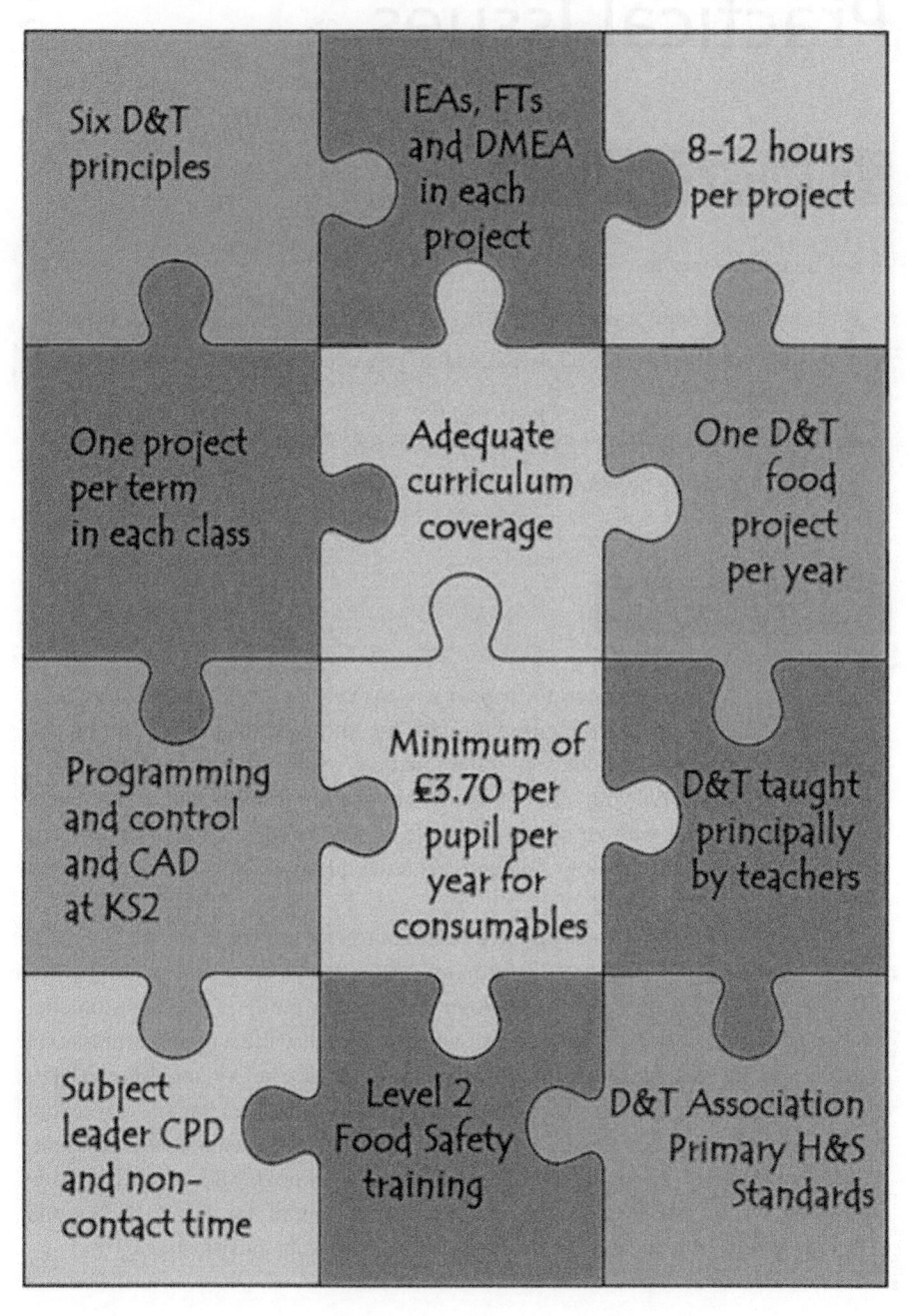

Six D&T principles	IEAs, FTs and DMEA in each project	8–12 hours per project
One project per term in each class	Adequate curriculum coverage	One D&T food project per year
Programming and control and CAD at KS2	Minimum of £3.70 per pupil per year for consumables	D&T taught principally by teachers
Subject leader CPD and non-contact time	Level 2 Food Safety training	D&T Association Primary H&S Standards

Minimum Requirements for effective practice in KS1 and KS2

Let us start by considering the 'bare minimum' as identified by the Design and Technology Association Expert Subject Advisory Group for primary schools (Figure 8.1 shows their 'jigsaw diagram'). Be aware that this really is the 'bare minimum' not the complacent 'what we can get away with' list. The online link to this document can be found in the Recommended Reading list at the end of this chapter. A checklist has been given with the diagram, which can provide a useful self-assessment tool for schools or individual teachers.

> **Pause for thought**
>
> What would you regard as 'minimum requirements' for yourself to be effectively teaching design and technology in the classroom? To what extent do you consider you have achieved these? Make a list of your achievements and an 'action plan' list for developing your knowledge, competence and confidence.
>
> What would you regard as 'minimum requirements' for a school to be delivering design and technology effectively?
>
> Without being judgemental, students on school placement might like to attempt to complete this for the school in which they are placed and then discuss their perceptions with the design and technology subject leader. There is probably more going on than a student can observe within a short period in a school but on final placement students should be discussing with subject leaders such things as long-term action plans, budget constraints and leadership issues – and this diagram is a good place to start.

The following are some brief comments and weblinks related to each piece of the jigsaw:

1. *Each project should address the six D&T principles* of the 'star diagram' (Fig. 1.3 in Chapter 1), as explained in https://www.data.org.uk/media/1130/school-curriculum-principles-for-dt.pdf
2. *Investigative and Evaluative Activities (IEAs), Focused Tasks (FTs) and a Design, Make and Evaluate Assignment (DMEA) should* be included in each design and technology project (see Chapter 2). These three kinds of activities were introduced in the 1995 National Curriculum and remain the basis of the planners in the Design and Technology Association's Projects on a Page, free to members or purchasable through the Association's website.
3. *8–12 hours per project.* This works out to between 40 and 60 minutes per week, but it does not mean the subject has to be taught every week. Many schools prefer to allocate a whole afternoon a week to design and technology in one half-term and to art and design in the next. Some schools prefer to block their design and technology teaching into a 'D&T Week'. Care is needed with this

kind of planning as it can minimize opportunities for making connections between design and technology and other subjects. For instance, there is considerable benefit in running science and technology projects together, especially for areas such as mechanisms or electrical control. Likewise, a project involving textiles, such as bag-making, could span both art and technology.

4. *One project per term in each class*: This means 3 projects per year; 18 projects across KS1 and KS2. Although many counties work on the 3-term year (10–12 week terms), some counties (e.g. Kent) work on a 6-term system. So think 3 projects per year.

5. *Curriculum coverage* = KS1: food, textiles, structures, mechanisms and KS2: food, textiles, structures, mechanical systems, electrical/electronic systems. See Chapter 4.

6. *Teach one food project per year,* including cooking and nutrition requirements. This means that 6 out of the 18 projects across KS1 and KS2 in order to meet the requirement of more than one dish in KS1 and a range of dishes in KS2. Each project must meet National Curriculum requirements for designing and making, not just the cooking and nutrition. Some schools or classes (especially KS1 and Early Years classes) may prefer to teach cooking in small groups on a weekly rota. In this case, ensure that all children have 8–12 hours' food experience per year (i.e. one project allocation of hours).

7. *During KS2 teach programming and control in two D&T projects and computer-aided design (CAD) in two D&T projects*. Four of the twelve D&T projects in KS2 should include computer/electronic control. This is one of the areas that the National Curriculum writers were keen to include in order to extend the experience of children in KS2. Many schools are confident in teaching children to make electrical circuits and now need to devise ways of applying this into real projects and to extend this into electronic control. The Design and Technology Association's guidance materials are available at https://www.data.org.uk/shop-products/applying-computing-in-dt-at-ks2-and-ks3/

8. *Minimum budget for consumables* in KS1 and KS2 – £3.70 per pupil per year (at February 2016 prices). The Design and Technology Association's Projects on a Page were written to this budget. There is, however, a long 'exclusion list': items that would be in general stock such as glue, paper or card, plus 'one off' purchases 'for which a further budget would need to be allocated', such as tools, equipment, utensils, construction kits, product handling collections, teaching aids, computer hardware and software.

> **Pause for thought**
>
> Does this sound like a reasonable amount? Would you have expected it to be more or less? How do schools acquire additional funding for expensive or ambitious projects? To what extent does a school known to you depend on donations of consumable resources from parents or local industry/commerce?

Design and technology requires consumable resources, some of which are expensive. Teachers have to work within the resources available in the school. For instance, there is no point planning a project requiring 4 wooden wheels, an electric motor, 2 AA batteries and a battery holder plus wire per child in a class of 30 if this has not been allocated for in this year's budget. When I was subject leader in a first school (which taught children from Year R to Year 4), I divided the available budget equally between the 5-year groups and suggested they devise three schemes of work (one for each term) of which:

- One used mainly recycled resources (including such things as electric motors which were reused year on year),
- One used mainly resources that came from general stock (such as paper and card),
- One required special or more expensive consumable resources (such as the wooden wheels),
- tools and equipment,
- a wish-list.

9 *D&T should be taught principally by teachers.* This is to counter a trend for design and technology to be covered by teaching assistants during teachers' release time or for the subject to be taught to small groups of children by a teaching assistant or visitor. Design and technology, like every other subject of the curriculum, needs to be taught by someone who has properly studied the principles, pedagogy and practice.

The Design and Technology Association lists the following reasons: *'to (a) ensure the ongoing development of [teachers'] subject expertise (b) maximise links between D&T and other subjects such as mathematics, science or art and design (c) help to ensure safe practice (d) build on children's previous learning and (e) make sure the subject is afforded the same status as other National Curriculum subjects.'*

This does not mean, however, that teachers have to teach design and technology on their own in the classroom. An extra pair of hands or a visiting expert is always welcome but teaching the subject effectively is the teacher's responsibility.

10 *Subject leader – entitlement to CPD and non-contact time.* The School Teachers' Pay and Conditions Document 2015 (paragraph 54.6) states that subject leaders are entitled to a reasonable amount of time during school sessions for the purpose of discharging their responsibilities. This means that they should have time to help and advise you when you are on school placement, in your NQT (newly qualified teacher) year and beyond.

11 & 12 *Health and safety:* The Design and Technology Association recommends that at least one member of staff attends their Level 2 Food Safety training, gains accreditation and disseminates this training to colleagues. The Design and Technology Association is not the only provider but ensure that any course offered will lead to accreditation at Level 2 – especially if cheaper! Likewise,

the Design and Technology Association recommends that at least one member of staff attends their Primary Health and Safety Standards training, gains accreditation and subsequently disseminates this training to colleagues. Again, check the accreditation offered by other providers and also check that guidelines offered comply with your local authority's, employer's and/or school's guidance on health and safety. The following section provides only general guidance on where to find information.

> **Pause for thought**
>
> When on school placement do/did you know who had received this training in health and safety? How is health and safety information and guidance disseminated in a school known to you? If you volunteer in a school, are on placement or work in a teaching or teaching assistant capacity, make sure you find out this essential information.

Health and safety

The document most frequently referred to with regard to health and safety issues when teaching design and technology is *Be safe!*, published by the Association for Science *(4th edition, 2011)*.

CLEAPSS (www.cleapss.org.uk) is the organization that specifies and advises on safe storage and use of a range of tools, equipment and materials in schools (including glues and other chemicals). Despite having the words 'secondary' and 'science' in the link, this leads you direct to the 'Health and Safety in Primary Science and Technology' guidance: http://www.cleapss.org.uk/attachments/article/0/PS22.pdf?Secondary/Science/Guidance%20Leaflets/?New%20teachers/

This guidance includes the following reassurance: *'How safe are primary science and technology? Very safe, although there are some hazards, associated with:*

- *sharp objects such as tools and glass;*
- *flames and hot things (hot water, glue guns, etc.);*
- *equipment powered by mains electricity;*
- *chemicals (including "kitchen" chemicals);*
- *animal and plant specimens;*
- *microorganisms.'*

Thus, the CLEAPSS document assesses the risks involved in teaching design and technology as *'insignificant'* and that *'with careful preparation and sensible precautions, accidents seldom occur'*. As for health risks, the same document assesses these as *'Virtually none'*.

The East Sussex Education Authority has published a very useful 'Design Technology Code of Practice – Primary Schools', available at https://czone.eastsussex.gov.uk/schoolmanagement/healthsafety/curriculum/pages/DesignTechnology-healthandsafetydocuments.aspx

It refers to the 'Be Safe' guidance booklet published by CLEAPSS and provides a summary of such issues as risk assessment, supervision, purchasing and storing resources and materials, training and monitoring.

The National Union of Teachers also provides guidance in their leaflet 'Safety in Practical Lessons', available at https://www.teachers.org.uk/help-and-advice/health-and-safety/s/safety-practical-lessons

This organization offers insurance for teachers against injury to themselves or pupils. Rather than offering clear 'do's and don'ts' the NUT document states: *'Although some activities are inherently more hazardous than others, all practical activities can become hazardous in some circumstances due to factors such as pupil misbehaviour, poorly designed work areas, inexperience of teachers, ability of pupils, etc.'*

This is a good point. A class of children is not exactly like the class next door; the class you had last year were not the same as those you have now or will teach next year. I once had a Year 3 class with whom I had to pretend to myself that I normally allowed children to talk through the register or we would have not got any further that day; the following year I had the kind of class where if I just said 'I think someone is talking in here' and a deathly hush would descend. Later, when I was teaching Year 1, I was due to receive a class that included a child who had the cognitive maturity of a two-year-old. Everything even vaguely hazardous went up on top of the cupboards including scissors (his favourite throwing device) and spare pencils. The most challenging child I ever taught would probably have stabbed us all with the sharp knives in the cooking area had he known they were there – yet for years classes of children had queued there waiting to go into the hall for lunch and stared disinterestedly at knives lying on the draining board.

The National Union of Teachers recommends that some form of risk assessment should appear on every scheme of work/lesson plan in which practical activity will take place. This might be a generic comment or brief note but there should always be an outline of the principle risks and the measures (to be) taken to reduce or remove those risks. For instance, although low-level risk would be expected for a lesson making pop-up greetings cards, a lesson in which groups of children would be doing batik with a teaching assistant in a corridor area outside the classroom would obviously need a much greater consideration of health and safety – and this would all need to be recorded on the lesson plan.

The age, quality, maintenance and repair of tools and equipment need to be considered, including their suitability for the age group of the pupils. Protective clothing must be available and used – including such measures as tying back hair and removing jewellery if appropriate. The suitability of the teaching area needs to be taken into consideration, especially the siting of potentially hazardous tools and equipment. Think about trailing electrical leads – and no extension leads to be used, ever!

Inclusion and diversity

Although the profile of mainstream school primary pupils represents almost the whole range of the population, the profiles of school can be remarkably different to each other. However, all pupils are entitled to have access to the National Curriculum, fitted to their own capacities and capabilities.

Teachers and trainees should seek guidance from the Special Educational Needs Coordinator (SENCo) over any activity or pupil about which they feel concerned, whether this is connected with the pupil's capability or behaviour. Support should be in place to enable the pupil (and the rest of the class) to maximize their learning and enjoyment of the lesson. It can be disheartening for other pupils to realize that their class is being restricted in the opportunities provided because of so-and-so's behaviour. This can easily escalate into resentment, ostracism and possibly bullying. It can also significantly interfere with other pupils' access to the full national curriculum.

The phrase 'behaviour for learning' should be your guiding principle: what is the appropriate behaviour required for everyone to benefit from this lesson? Clear behavioural boundaries will need to be stated at the start of any potentially hazardous activity, with penalties equally clearly stated. In extreme circumstances, prior arrangements may need to be made for escorting a pupil elsewhere if his or her actions become a danger or hindrance to others. A design and technology lesson can too quickly become an unsafe environment; you cannot take the risk of major challenges to your teacherly authority. I once observed a student on placement in a Year 5 class trying to teach her first food technology lesson: designing foods for a new take-away planning to open in the locality. 'Now, I'm Miss Take' she said brightly. 'Ha, ha! You're a mistake' said some wag and she'd lost it. Think first before scoring own goals such as this.

Trainees on placement in a school must follow the procedures in place in that school, regardless of whether or not these conform to their own style or preference. I used to frequently visit a school with a fairly challenging clientele. The school's behavioural strategy was: first offence > 'action replay' (child states what they should have been doing and goes and does it); second offence > orange card (as action replay but name goes on white board); third offence (as action replay and child is removed from activity). I observed so many students not following this pattern and floundering simply because they were not acting like a teacher as the pupils in that school understood that to be.

However, not all children with special educational needs pose such an obvious threat to the smooth flow of your lessons. You might have a child who is an elective mute (they never speak in school) or has a hearing or visual impairment. You need to ensure the health and safety of these pupils within a potentially hazardous environment. Check: Do they understand that the cooker is hot? Do they know that the glue gun is plugged in and switched on? If the child has difficulty understanding such issues, ensure they are kept well away from danger. Site any potentially hazardous process, equipment or materials well away from where they are working and ensure they are supervised at all times. Children who have mobility problems may also pose a risk to themselves and others around potentially hazardous tools and equipment, just by not being completely stable on their feet and having the tendency to grab at things when they wobble.

There seems to be more guidance around for supporting children with emotional, behavioural or cognitive difficulties than for supporting those with physical difficulties. Help is available, however, from charities, societies and support groups for specific disabilities such as paraplegia, spina bifida or cerebral palsy. A specific challenge is posed in the case of children who are regressing or becoming more disabled with the passing of time, for instance, sufferers of muscular dystrophy. This is an issue of ensuring quality of life for a child who may already be intuitively aware that his or her time is short. Organizing the classroom so that pupils with physical disabilities can have maximum access to the curriculum and to the practical activity in which their peers are engaged is absolutely vital. One of my colleagues rearranged her classroom so that all practical equipment such as scissors, rulers and glue were right by a pupil's place at the back of the room by the fire exit – his means of getting in and out of the classroom avoiding steps. A simple and practical solution in supporting a child who needed to get the best out of his time.

When I had a child join my Year 1 class who had Asperger's Syndrome, his learning support assistant assumed I would be the 'expert' simply because I was a teacher. She was surprised to learn that he was the first child with this condition that I had ever taught and that I was relying on her expertise, especially for practical subjects like design and technology where there would be a lot of movement and noise in different parts of the classroom. We quickly established a routine in which I briefed her on what would happen in the lesson and then she was able to explain to him what to expect by creating a sequence of pictures. If I needed to change plans, I needed to remember to tell her first so that she could inform him. Her success was underlined to me some years later when I called by the school one afternoon when an after-school technology club was in full swing. The teacher running the club said 'Can you remember who that is?' pointing out a boy completely absorbed in the work of his group. It was this boy, now aged nine, no longer needing the sequences of pictures; telling him was enough.

One group of pupils who often struggle with academic subjects but who thrive in design and technology are dyslexics. This is because they usually have a very well-developed spatial sense. Many architects and engineers are dyslexic. They are extremely good at imagining a structure from many different viewpoints (including inside out) and can see how parts and systems are connected or interact with each other. Take the opportunity to praise and value their prowess and buoy up their self-esteem.

Finally, a group of pupils whose needs are often overlooked but for whom certain practical activities are difficult due to a lack of tools and equipment that they can use effectively are left-handers.

> **Pause for thought**
>
> What difficulties does being left-handed raise when doing practical activities in design and technology? Check these out with a left-handed friend or family member (or reflect on your own experiences if you are left-handed).

> Benson and Bond addressed the difficulties of being left-handed in design and technology lessons in a paper delivered at the PATT32 Conference in the Netherlands (PATT = Pupils' Attitudes Towards Technology). The link to their paper is given in the Recommended Reading list at the end of this chapter – but note that this link is to the whole conference proceedings; Benson and Bond's paper begins at page 95.

Developing your professional knowledge in design and technology

Throughout your career, you need to maintain your commitment to ongoing professional development. If you care about your pupils' progress in design and technology then you will keep up to date with current developments, as well as maintaining and developing your own knowledge, skills and understanding of the subject. If you have carefully and thoughtfully read all the chapters in this book, you should have enough theoretical understanding to teach the subject but to be really effective in the classroom you also need to develop your practical knowledge. It is difficult to teach the subject well if you have little experience or confidence in practical hands-on designing and making. Begin with making the things that you want your pupils to make. You should do this as preparation for your lessons anyway or else you will not know if your ideas will work or what the pitfalls are. Once when I had planned making paper beads with Year 2, I had imagined them winding the paper around a thin stick but a quick bit of experimenting at home revealed that the hole through the centre would be far too small for a child to thread the yarn through just with their fingers. The answer was to wind the paper around a pencil.

The Design and Technology Association runs courses for teachers and many university faculties of education also run courses for teachers in local schools, which may also lead to Masters level credits. You may find that there are informal courses in your local area, perhaps organized through your local education authority. If your school is part of a cluster or academy trust, then practical courses may be arranged through these. If not, then why not be the one to suggest that this would be helpful? This demonstrates your commitment to your ongoing professional development. If you feel that the few hours you had on your initial teaching course were barely enough to help you begin to teach design and technology effectively, then make sure you put this on your developmental targets list. It is all too easy to think that these targets should always focus on English, mathematics and science (and these, obviously, are very important) but you need to be able to teach the other subjects well too. In terms of career development, choosing to specialize in a subject where other people struggle is a wise move. You quickly become known as someone that others can turn to for advice and help.

The Design and Technology Association has published a 'Primary Self-Review Framework' to guide schools through the important issues. It is aimed at subject leaders but much of what they say applies equally to class teachers. The chapters cover the following topics:

- Curriculum Planning (nature of the subject; long- and medium-term planning)
- Teaching and Learning (progression, assessment, quality teaching in the EYFS, KS1 and KS2)
- Leadership
- Resources and safety (tools, equipment, teaching resources, health and safety)

This tabulated document lists the important principles of each topic and provides direct links to the Design and Technology Association's publications that provide the relevant information.

For instance:

'Teachers plan a range of real and relevant contexts for designing and making.'
Links to:

- the 2016 Design and Technology Primary Subject Leaders' file Section 3.2: Principles of curriculum planning;
- the Design and Technology Association's Projects on a Page;
- National Curriculum 2014 programmes of study;
- the Design and Technology Association's Annotated Programme of Study – Key messages and explanatory notes for schools.

All primary schools should have a copy of the Primary Subject Leaders' file. If not, suggest that they buy it. This is an absolutely invaluable document, recently updated to conform to the 2014 National Curriculum. Faced with an inspector, a subject leader or class teacher can confidently say that they are using this file as the basis for their curriculum development. If, when you read the file, you feel that you or your school has a long way to go, then devise a realistic action plan. Discuss the plan with the subject leader or senior management team. Then, the following term or year, you can identify your progress and set another realistic target. Such clear plans for your own professional development and the development of design and technology in your classroom, year group and/or school will begin to mark you out as someone who is well-focused, organized and going places! The last thing you want is for someone in management to say 'How is design and technology in your classroom?' or (worse) 'When we last met, we discussed design and technology; how have you ensured you have made progress on those issues?' and you are left mumbling in your boots because you have not done anything and were secretly hoping they would have forgotten about it and ask about something else.

Today's teaching world is one in which you have to set yourself clear targets for everything and be seen to be working towards them. Get your action plans sorted – and even make action plans of action plans! Then you can say to senior management 'This term I am working on this; next term I plan to address this, and by the end of the year I should be well on the way towards that.' And maybe even 'I'm having to put this other issue on the back burner for now, but it is on the top of the list for next year.' When I was teaching in a primary school, as well as being a Year Leader, I was also subject leader for three curriculum subjects (including design and technology). I found that drawing up action plans was the only way I could keep on top of everything and prioritize what I would focus on developing each term.

What if I'm asked to be design and technology subject leader?

> **Pause for thought**
>
> How would you react if you were asked to be the design and technology subject leader? Does the idea of leading any subject across the whole school scare you or just design and technology? Or is this progression in your personal career development plan? Would it be design and technology you would want to lead? If not, why not?

Hopefully, your reaction would be to be delighted and say 'Yes, certainly – but please can I go on a subject leaders' course?'

Maybe design and technology was not your specialist subject at university; maybe you do not even have a GCSE in the subject. Being a good subject leader does not necessarily depend on your prior knowledge. Half-remembered facts and procedures from years ago may actually get in the way of developing your knowledge and understanding of the current developments in the subject. In any case, what you learnt to do for your GCSE is of doubtful relevance in the primary school; younger pupils are not putting together a portfolio to pass an exam, they are learning to design and make pleasing products that work well and satisfy the needs and wants of a familiar user. As stated above, the Design and Technology Association provides the help, support and documentation that you will need. If you want to talk to someone, you can ring them up and they will put a primary advisor in touch with you. The STEM organization also has local groups but, in my experience, they tend to consist mainly of secondary science teachers – but it may be different in your area. Clusters of schools often have meetings of subject leaders for each subject and this will enable you to meet colleagues from other schools and benefit from their expertise.

Look for as much support as you can get but remember that your senior management team have seen your potential and believe you can do it – and so you can. Take a deep breath, download everything you can for free from the Design and Technology Association's website and provide your budget holder with a list of all the publications you want the school to buy (with justification for the purchase).

The first things you need to do is:

- Look at all long- and medium-term plans across the whole school – check them against those key principles on the 'star diagram';
- Check that there are sufficient tools, equipment and materials available for each year group to satisfy the requirements of the National Curriculum.

Then:

Meet with each Year Group or Key Stage leader and discuss how the subject can be moved forward – be diplomatic: what do they need, how could you support them, do they understand the requirements of the National Curriculum 2014, do they know of the 'star diagram'? Devise an action plan with them. The medium-term plans they have in place already may just need some tweaking or they may want a total revision. Remember the Design and Technology Association's Projects on a Page. Would these solve the problem? Perhaps just looking at the structure of these would help some colleagues to re-structure their own ideas, whereas others might decide that adopting one or more of these projects would save a lot of time and effort.

Complete the cycle by writing your action plan based on all the feedback and agreements made with colleagues. What needs doing, how will you schedule this (realistically – you cannot do everything at once and you cannot expect your colleagues to either). Arrange a meeting with the overall curriculum leader for your Key Stage or school to share your plans, both long-term goals and short-term action items. Get a yearly cycle going of discussion with Year Groups/Key Stage leaders and reporting back to senior management.

Arrange to have a 'state of the subject' (celebration plus planned progress) reporting back to all staff and governors on an annual basis. A good idea here is to have a display in a public space (e.g. the school library) to which governors and parents can be invited, followed by tea and cakes for staff and governors, after which you can present your 'progress and plans' report. Having seen all the wonderful work the children have done, the feel-good fairy will (hopefully) wave her wand and you will be most warmly congratulated and get all the support and budget to move the subject forward. Take plenty of photos and write up the event for the school newsletter/website, and tie it into your subject development plan to put in your folder for Ofsted and for your career development, CV and future job applications!

> **Pause for thought**
>
> *Could you do this?*
> Probably not right away and you would want at least one year's full-time teaching behind you before you are ready to take on a new challenge. Try to avoid taking on new responsibilities and start teaching a different year group all at the same time.
> *Actually, the correct question is: could you learn to do this?*
> The answer to this should be, probably yes! You won't go into the role knowing everything but enthusiasm, commitment and a willingness to learn and develop your knowledge and capability is all that is required to begin to take responsibility across the whole school. Your senior management team is there to support you in your new role, so make sure you avail yourself of it.

Summary

This final chapter has looked at three practical areas related to managing the teaching of design and technology

- the help available from the Design and Technology Association;
- health and safety guidance from a range of sources;
- inclusion issues that relate directly to participation in practical activities.

The chapter concluded with the challenge: what if they ask you to be the design and technology subject leader? To which my reply is: *why not you*?

Recommended reading

Benson, C. and Bond, R. (2016). 'I can't see how to do it': Left handed pupils – are their needs being met in design and technology in primary settings? In de Vries, M., Bekker-Holtland, A. and van Dijk, G. (eds.) *Technology Education for 21st Century Skills, PATT-32 Proceedings;* Netherlands; ITEEA. Available at https://www.iteea.org/File.aspx?id=39504&v=76e4030

Design and Technology Association (2016). Minimum Requirements for Effective Practice; available at https://www.data.org.uk/shop-products/minimum-requirements-for-effective-practice-in-ks1-and-ks2/

Association for Science Education (2011). *Be Safe! Health and Safety in School Science and Technology for Teachers of 3–12 Year Olds* (4th ed.). Herts., England: Association for Science Education.

In summary

For Effective and Creative Teaching of Design and Technology.....................

You do not need to know how to do everything! You do need to understand the principles of Design and Technology education and know what effective teaching of the subject looks like. If you have not been able to observe design and technology lessons during your Initial Teacher Education course, make it a priority to consult your subject leader and observe him or her teaching. Ask questions about pedagogy, then research the practical aspects of your lessons as you plan them. You can learn plenty of tips from other teachers and from various websites on how to make things as you go along.

Be sure you understand the National Curriculum for England or its equivalent in your country – This is ultimately what your teaching is going to be measured against. Make sure you understand the principles underlying it, not just the list of skills for each age group.

Before the lesson – Always practise anything you are going to ask children to do, however simple it might seem in the instructions you found on a helpful website.

Health and Safety – Make sure there is adequate supervision for any techniques and tools that might present hazards to children's safety. Be organized about setting out and putting away materials and equipment. Clearly state class rules about safe working practices before children start any practical work. Do not be afraid to stop children from using a particular equipment (or even stop the whole lesson) if you feel a situation is becoming dangerous.

Teach creatively and encourage the children's creativity – Vary the way you teach. Think about different approaches to designing. Do the children *need* to draw it? Would talking about it be better? Do they need to learn or practise some skills in order to make a successful product? Encourage children to make design choices and (as far as possible) decide what materials, techniques, size, shape, colour etc. they want their product to be. Do not, on any account, end up with a class set of identical products!

Encourage discussion – At all stages in designing and making a successful product, children need to discuss their ideas with you and with each other. Let them talk – but ensure the noise level is not hindering their discussions. Get involved on a one-to-one basis in discussing children's ideas and the progress of their work. Suggest and demonstrate ways forward – they expect teachers to show them things and know better ways of working.

Do not be a loner – Use online resources and join chat forums; go on courses; get involved in local STEM and similar groups; join the Design and Technology Association (www.data.org.uk).

Have fun! Research has shown that children really enjoy Design and Technology!

Bibliography

Benson, C and Lunt, J. (2011). *International Handbook of Primary Technology Education: Reviewing the Past Twenty Years*. Rotterdam, Netherlands: Sense Publishers.

British Nutritional Foundation Framework of Core Competencies. Available at https://www.nutrition.org.uk/foodinschools/competences/competences.html

Bruner, J. (1985). *Actual Minds, Possible Worlds*. New York: Harvard University Press.

Bruner, J.E. (1985). 'Narrative & Paradigmatic Modes of Thought.' In Eisner, E. (ed.), *Learning & Teaching the Ways of Knowing*. Chicago: NSSE U.S.A.

Cross, N. (2001). 'Designerly ways of knowing: Design discipline versus design science.' *Design Issues*, 17 (3), pp. 49–55. Available at: http://oro.open.ac.uk/3281/1/Designerly-_DisciplinevScience.pdf

Cross, N. (2006). *Designerly Ways of Knowing*. London: Springer-Verlag

Csikszentmihalyi, M. (1990). *Flow: The psychology of optimal experience* (1st ed.). New York: Harper & Row

Dawkins, R. (1989). The Selfish Gene (2nd ed.). Oxford: Oxford University Press

Department of Education (2013). *Design and Technology Programmes of Study for Key Stages 1 and 2; National Curriculum in England*. London: Department of Education, London. Available at https://www.gov.uk/government/uploads/system/uploads/attachment_data/file/239041/PRIMARY_national_curriculum_-_Design_and_technology.pdf

Department of Education, Pretoria (2002). *South Africa National Curriculum for technology: Revised National Curriculum Statement Grades R-9 (Schools Technology)*; Pretoria, South Africa; Department of Education. Available at http://www.education.gpg.gov.za/Document5/Documents/Intermediate%20Phase%20Technology.pdf

Design and Technology Association. *Minimum Requirements for Effective Practice*. Available at: https://www.data.org.uk/shop-products/minimum-requirements-for-effective-practice-in-ks1-and-ks2/

Design and Technology Association. *Principles of Design and Technology*. Available at: https://www.data.org.uk/media/1130/school-curriculum-principles-for-dt.pdf

Design and Technology Association and National Curriculum Expert Group for D&T (2013). *Characteristics of a Genuine D&T Experience within the School Curriculum: Principles for Guiding and Evaluating Practice*. Wellesbourne: Design and Technology Association. Available at: https://www.data.org.uk/media/1130/school-curriculum-principles-for-dt.pdf

Design and Technology Association: Progression Framework https://www.data.org.uk/resource-shop/primary/design-and-technology-progression-framework/ Formative assessment https://www.data.org.uk/resource-shop/primary/formative-assessment-initial-guidance/

De Vries, M. (2016). *Teaching about Technology: An Introduction to the Philosophy of Technology for Non-philosophers* (2nd ed.). Switzerland: Springer International

Donaldson (1992). *Human Minds: An Exploration*. Allen Lane: The Penguin Press.

Flinn, E. (2016). *The Really Useful Primary Design and Technology*. London: Routledge.

Gardner, H. (1983). *Frames of Mind: The Theory of Multiple Intelligences*. New York: Basic Books.

Grainger, T. Barnes, J. and Scoffham, S. (2004). A Creative Cocktail Creative Teaching in Initial Teacher Education. *Journal of Education and Teaching*, 30 (3).

Hope, G. (2004). *Teaching Design & Technology 3-11*. London: Continuum Publishers

Hope (2005). The Types of Drawings that Young Children Produce in Response to Design Tasks. In *Design and Technology Education: An International Journal 10, 1*; Design and Technology Association. Wellesbourne: Warwickshire. Available at https://ojs.lboro.ac.uk/ojs/index.php/DATE/article/view/Journal_10.1_2005_RES3/112

Hope, G. (2006). *Teaching Design and Technology in Key Stages 1 and 2*. Exeter: Learning Matters.

Hope, G. (2009). Designer species: human uniqueness and its educational implications. In Norman, E. and Spendlove, D. (eds). *The Design and Technology Association International Research Conference 2009*. Wellesbourne: The Design and Technology Association, pp. 53–8.

Howe, A., Davies, D. and Ritchie, R. (2001). *Primary Design and Technology for the Future: Creativity, Culture and Citizenship*. David Fulton Publishers (republished 2012 by Routledge)

Keirl, S. (2002). Hedgehogs, Foxes, Crows and other 'intelligent' beings: Explorations of the Relationship Between Multiple Intelligence Theory and Design and Technology. Available at http://research.gold.ac.uk/9655/1/0380208TERCmi%26D%26T.pdf

Kimbell, R. /SEC/OU(1986) *Craft, Design and Technology*. Buckinghamshire: The Open University Press.

Kimbell, R., Stabels, K., Lawler, T. and Woziak, T. (1991). Assessment and Performance Unit Design and Technology. Available at https://www.stem.org.uk/rxzdq

McLain, M., McLain, M., Tsai, J., Martin, M., Bell, D. and woof, D. (2016). *Traditional Tales and Imaginary Contexts in Primary Design and Technology: A Case Study*. Available at: https://repository.edgehill.ac.uk/8921/1/Traditional%20tales%20and%20imaginary%20contexts%20in%20primary%20design%20and%20technolog%20%20.pdf

Middleton, H. (2000). Design and Technology: What is the Problem?. In Kimbell, R. (ed.) Design and Technology International Millennium Conference. Wellesbourne, Warwickshire: The Design and Technology Association. Available at https://dspace.lboro.ac.uk/dspace-jspui/handle/2134/3423

Ministry of Education, New Zealand: The New Zealand National Curriculum for technology: http://nzcurriculum.tki.org.nz/The-New-Zealand-Curriculum/Technology

Ministry of Education, Ontario, Canada Science and Technology (2007). Available at http://www.edu.gov.on.ca/eng/curriculum/elementary/scientec18currb.pdf

Ministry of Education and Employment (2012). *National Curriculum Framework*. Valetta, Malta: Ministry of Education & Employment. Available at https://education.gov.mt/en/Documents/A%20National%20Curriculum%20Framework%20for%20All%20-%202012.pdf

Newton, D. (2005). Teaching Design and Technology 3–11. London: Scholastic Publishers.

Owen-Jackson, G. and Rutland, M. (2016). Food in the school curriculum in England: Its development from cookery to cookery. In *Design and Technology Education: An International Journal*, 21 (3). Available at https://ojs.lboro.ac.uk/ojs/index.php/DATE/article/view/2159

Parkinson, E. and Hope, G. (2011). Children, Construction and Technological Literacy. In Stables, K., Benson, C. and de Vries, M. (2011). *Perspectives on Learning in Design and Technology Education, Proceedings of the PATT25:CRIPT8 Conference, London, July 1-5 2011*, Technology Education Research Unit, Goldsmiths, University of London.

Parkinson, E. F. and Hope, G. (2008). 'Design across the Curriculum: expanding opportunities for pupil agency and creativity'. Available at www.leeds.ac.uk/educol/documents/178008.doc

Rapley, J. (2016). *Project Template*; private communication; Meadows School, Kent

Religious Education Council for England and Wales (2013). Curriculum Framework for Religious Education in England. Available at http://resubjectreview.recouncil.org.uk/media/file/RE_Review_Summary.pdf

Roberts, P., Archer, B. and Baynes, K. (1991). *Modelling the Language of Design*. Available at https://dspace.lboro.ac.uk/dspace-jspui/bitstream/2134/1689/3/roberts_archer_baynes.pdf

Rogers, M. and Clare, D. (1994). *The Process Diary: Developing Capability within National Curriculum Design & Technology – some initial findings*; International Design and Technology Educational Research Conference, 1994; Loughborough University of Technology, Department of Design & Technology. Available at https://dspace.lboro.ac.uk/dspace-jspui/handle/2134/1548

Ryle, G. (1949). *The Concept of Mind*. London: Hutchinson.

South Australia Curriculum Standards and Accountability (2004). *South Australian Companion Document for Design and Technology*; The State of South Australia, Department of Education and Children's Services. Available at http://www.sacsa.sa.edu.au/ATT/%7BF51C47E3-B6F3-4765-83C3-0E27FF5DD952%7D/R-10_Design_&_Tech.pdf

Index

art and design 9–10, 13–14, 34, 64
assessment (by pupils) 15, 18, 56–7, 72, 140–1
assessment (for learning) 15, 72, 134–5, 144–6, 147
assessment (of teaching) 135–8
authenticity 5, 15, 18, 40, 41, 71–3, 91

British Nutritional Council framework 30

child development 16, 17–19
computer control 84
computing (NC subject) 34–5
construction kits 9, 6, 70, 74–5, 90, 98, 100, 102–3, 106
continuing professional development 158–61
cooking 29–30, 35, 48, 57, 152
creative teaching 57, 64–5, 135–8
creativity 14, 16–17, 19, 49, 54–6, 107, 119, 113, 115, 118–19
cross-curricular links 30–40, 64–5, 119–20, 129–31

defining design and technology 5, 7–15, 46–7, 163
defining technology 11–12
Design and Technology Association 13, 15, 21, 30, 35, 144, 150–4, 158–9
design brief 5, 70–2, 118–19, 121
design capability 19, 97, 115–18
design criteria 5, 56, 68
design processes 16, 49–54
drawing 47, 56–9, 87–9

Early Years 3–4, 101–2, 114
electrical control 83–4
empathy 16, 19
English (NC subject) 31–2
evaluating (own work) 15, 16, 140–1

fantasy 116–18
food 29–30, 59–62, 128–9, 152
functionality 15, 17, 71–3

gardening 59–62
geography (NC subject) 35, 89–91
glossary 5

health and safety 69, 154–5
history (NC subject) 35–8, 73, 129–31
history (of design and technology as NC subject) 22–4, 49–54
history of technology 1, 14, 36–8

inclusion and diversity 156–8
independence 138–9
international perspectives 40–2, 120–1
investigating existing products 121–8
iterative nature of designing 5, 26, 29, 47–9

Key Stage 1 39–40, 61–5, 77–8, 87–9, 115–19
Key Stage 2 27, 29, 33–4, 78–87, 126–7, 140–4
knowledge 19

left-handed pupils 157–8
local environment 125–8

making 75–86, 98–9
manipulating 101–3
materials 14, 68–9
mathematics 32
mechanisms 77–83
mending 105
minimum requirements 149–54
model 5, 69–70
modelling 54–7, 89–90, 99–101
modifying 105–7

National Curriculum for design and technology 1989 22
National Curriculum for design and technology 2004 22–4
National Curriculum for design and technology 2014 21, 27, 28–30

Ofsted reports 25–7, 133

planning for teaching 64–5, 91, 134–5, 138–9
play 95–6, 106, 115–18
problem-solving 53–4
process skills 94–6, 108–10
product collections 121–3
product (making) 68–9, 96–139
progression 143–5

puppets 79–80
purpose 13–15, 69, 72–3, 94–5

QCA schemes of work 24

religious education 38–9

science 9, 14, 32–4
star diagram 15, 70–2, 135,
STEM 22, 27
structures 74–7

subject leadership 153, 160–1

talk 58–9
teaching assistant/helper 63, 136–7, 153
technological capability 19
textiles 84–7, 130–1
toys 123–6

user 15, 68, 72–3, 94–7

well-being 16, 45–7